Property and Trust Law in Taiwan

Property and Trust Law in Taiwan

Second Edition

Yun-chien Chang
Weitseng Chen
Ying-Chieh WU

This book was originally published as a monograph in the International Encyclopaedia of Laws/Property and Trust Law.

Founding Editor: Roger Blanpain
General Editor: Frank Hendrickx
Volume Editors: Alain Verbeke & Vincent Sagaert

Wolters Kluwer

Published by:
Kluwer Law International B.V.
PO Box 316
2400 AH Alphen aan den Rijn
The Netherlands
E-mail: lrs-sales@wolterskluwer.com
Website: www.wolterskluwer.com/en/solutions/kluwerlawinternational

Sold and distributed by:
Wolters Kluwer Legal & Regulatory U.S.
7201 McKinney Circle
Frederick, MD 21704
United States of America
E-mail: customer.service@wolterskluwer.com

ISBN 978-94-035-4840-1

e-Book: ISBN 978-94-035-4850-0
web-PDF: ISBN 978-94-035-4860-9

This title is available on www.kluwerlawonline.com

The Authors[*]

Photo credit: Cookie Tsai.

Prof. Yun-chien Chang is a Research Professor at Institutum Iurisprudentiae, Academia Sinica, Taiwan and serves as the Director of its Empirical Legal Studies Center. He was or will be a visiting professor at Cornell University, Columbia University, New York University, the University of Chicago, St. Gallen University, Hebrew University of Jerusalem, and Rotterdam Institute of Law and Economics. He has also conducted research at Free University of Berlin, University of Paris II, and University of Tokyo. His current academic interests focus on economic, empirical and comparative analysis of private law (particularly property law), as well as empirical studies of the judicial system. Prof. Chang has authored and co-authored more than 100 journal articles and book chapters. His English articles have appeared in leading journals in the world, such as *Journal of Legal Studies*; *Journal of Legal Analysis*; *Journal of Law and Economics; American Law and Economics Review*; *Journal of Law, Economics, and Organization*; *Journal of Empirical Legal Studies*; *International Review of Law and Economics*; *European Journal of Law and Economics*; *I•Con*; *the University of Chicago Law Review*; *Notre Dame Law Review*; *Iowa Law Review* and the *Supreme Court Economic Review*, among others.

His monograph *Private Property and Takings Compensation: Theoretical Framework and Empirical Analysis* (Edward Elgar, 2013) was a winner of the Scholarly Monograph Award in the Humanities and Social Sciences. His second monograph in English, *Property Law: Comparative, Empirical, and Economic Analyses* (Cambridge University Press), is forthcoming in 2022. Prof. Chang (co-)edited *Empirical Legal Analysis: Assessing the Performance of Legal Institutions* (Routledge, 2014), *Law and Economics of Possession* (Cambridge University Press, 2015), *Private Law in China and Taiwan: Economic and Legal Analyses* (Cambridge University Press, 2016), and *Selection and Decision in Judicial Process Around the World: Empirical Inquires* (Cambridge University Press, 2020). Prof. Chang is also a co-author of *Property and Trust Law in Taiwan* (Wolters Kluwer, 2017; 2nd edition, 2022). He authored several books in

* We dedicate this book to Vicki Been, Robert Ellickson, Sheng-lin Jan（詹森林）, Tsung-jung Liu（劉宗榮）, Lionel Smith, William Swadling, Ming-Cheng Tsai（蔡明誠）, Frank Upham and Tay-Sheng Wang（王泰升）, who taught us property and trust law.

Chinese published in China and Taiwan, *Compensation for Physical and Regulatory Takings of Land: Theory and Practice* (Angle, 2013; 2nd edition, 2020), *Economic Analysis of Property Law* (Standard Chinese: Angle, 2015; 2nd edition, 2021; simplified Chinese: Beijing University Press, 2019), *Empirical Legal Studies: Empirical Legal Studies: Principles, Methods, and Applications* (New Sharing, 2019), and *Interpreting Private Law: A Social Scientific Approach* (New Sharing, 2020), and also (co-)edited *The Empirical Legal Studies Reader I: Domestic Perspectives* (The Law Press, 2020) and *Empirical Studies of the Judicial Systems 2011* (Institutum Iurisprudentiae, Academia Sinica; 2013).

Prof. Chang's academic achievements have won him the Career Development Award in 2016, Outstanding Scholar Award in 2016, Academia Sinica Law Journal Award in 2016, the Junior Research Investigators Award in 2015, the Best Poster Prize at 2011 CELS, and several research grants. He serves as a Co-Editor of *International Review of Law and Economics*; a Consultant Editor of *European Journal of Law and Economics*; an Editor of *Asian Journal of Comparative Law* and a Panelist on American Law Institute's *Restatement Fourth, Property* International Advisory Panel.

Prof. Chang received his J.S.D. and LL.M. degree from New York University School of Law, where he was also a Lederman/Milbank Law and Economics Fellow and a Research Associate at the Furman Center for Real Estate and Urban Policy, NYU. Before going to NYU, Prof. Chang had earned LL.B. and LL.M. degrees at National Taiwan University and passed the Taiwan bar. Prof. Chang has had working experience with prestigious law firms in Taiwan and has served as a legal assistant for the International Trade Commission.

More information: https://www.iias.sinica.edu.tw/member_post/5.

Weitseng Chen is an associate professor at National University of Singapore (NUS) Faculty of Law. He specializes in comparative Asian law—particularly within greater China area, with an emphasis on law and development, property law and financial institutions. Weitseng Chen received his JSD from Yale Law School where he was a Fulbright scholar. Thereafter, he worked for Stanford University as a Hewlett Fellow of the Center on Democracy, Development and the Rule of Law (CDDRL). Immediately before he joined NUS Faculty of Law, Weitseng Chen worked as a corporate lawyer at Davis Polk & Wardwell.

His recent research focuses on authoritarian legality, property rights transition in greater China, and Asian law & development. He has published the books entitled "*Beyond Regime Type: The Transformation of Police in Asia*" (w. Hualing Fu eds.) (Cambridge University Press, 2022), "*Authoritarian Legality in Asia: Formation, Development and Transition*" (Cambridge University Press, 2020) and "*The Beijing Consensus? How China Has Changed the Western Ideas of Law and Economic Development*" (Cambridge University Press, 2017). His other published articles can be found in the American Journal of Comparative Law, Journal of International Economic Law, Washington International Law Journal, Chicago Journal of International Law, Columbia Journal of Asian Law, and Australian Journal of Asian Law, etc.

Weitseng Chen has also held visiting academic appointments at Harvard Law School, Melbourne Law School, University of Tokyo, Seoul National University, University of Washington, University of British Columbia, Academia Sinica Institutum Iurisprudentiae, National Taiwan University, National Chengchi University, and FGV DIREITO SP Law School (Brazil). He is also a fellow of the Institute for Advanced Studies in Berlin (Wissenschaftskolleg zu Berlin).

Ying-Chieh WU (DPhil. *Oxon*) is an associate professor of Comparative Private Law at Seoul National University, School of Law (South Korea). Before joining SNU, he taught at National Taiwan University, College of Law (Taiwan), and Singapore Management University, School of Law (Singapore). He has taught and written in Korean, Chinese, English. Among his articles are "Unlocking Three Requirements of Real Subrogation" in *The Korean Journal of Civil Law* (2011, written in Korean), "Breach of Trust: Remedies and Their Legal Foundations" in *National Taiwan University Law Journal* (2015, written in Chinese), and "Trusts Reimagined: The Transplantation and Revolution of Trust Law in North East Asia" in *American Journal of Comparative Law* (2020, written in English). He also contributed to the books *Trust Law in Asian Civil Law Jurisdictions: A Comparative Analysis* (Lusina Ho & Rebecca Lee eds., Cambridge University Press, 2013), *Studies in the Contract Laws of Asia Vol. II Formation and Third-Party Beneficiaries* (Mindy C-Wishart et al. eds., Oxford University Press, 2018) *The Characterisation of Cryptocurrencies in Japan, South Korea and China*' in *The Private Law Implications of Cryptocurrencies* (David Fox &Sarah Green eds., Oxford University Press, 2019). He is the author of *Trust Law* (Hongmoonsa, Seoul 2021), and a monograph on comparative trust law (Cambridge University Press) and *Asia-Pacific Trusts Law: Adaptation in Context* (co-edited) will be published in 2022.

The Authors

Table of Contents

List of Abbreviations

CAA	Condominium Administration Act of Taiwan
CSTA	Chattels Security Transactions Act of Taiwan
DCFR	Draft Common Frame of Reference
LEA	Land Expropriation Act of Taiwan
TCC	Civil Code of Taiwan
TTA	Trust Act of Taiwan
TWD	Taiwan New Dollar

List of Abbreviations

Acknowledgments

We thank Wolters Kluwer for inviting us to write this monograph and Professor Wen Yeu Wang (National Taiwan University) for hooking the three authors together. Peter Chen and Neil Yang provided superb research assistance when we put together the final manuscript. We are equally grateful for the support from our home institutions—Academia Sinica, National University of Singapore (research fund no. R-241-000-122-112), and National Taiwan University, as well as the Ministry of Science and Technology in Taiwan, which financed Peter's internship. Chien-chang Huang, Chien-Chung Lin, and Lisa Wang also provided useful comments on English translation of Chinese legal terms.

Part of the contents in this monograph originally appeared in Yun-chien Chang's other academic works: "Condominium Law in Taiwan: Doctrinal Overview under the Lens of Information-Cost Theory," *Asia Pacific Law Review*, 23(2), 89–120 (2015); "Eminent Domain Law in Taiwan: New Law, Old Practice?," *Eminent Domain: A Comparative Perspective* (Iljoong Kim et al. eds, Cambridge University Press, 2017); "The Evolution of Property Law in Taiwan: An Unconventional Interest Group Story," *Private Law in China and Taiwan: Economic and Legal Analyses* (Yun-chien Chang et al. eds, Cambridge University Press, 2016).

Acknowledgments

General Introduction

§1. General Background of the Country

I. Geography

A. Geographic Location and Colonialism

1. Taiwan is an island located approximately 180 kilometers off the south-eastern coast of China. Having a total land mass of 35,883 square kilometers, Taiwan is smaller than Switzerland but larger than Belgium. Taiwan also lies between Northeast and Southeast Asia as it is just across mainland China from the Taiwan Strait. Such a location has made Taiwan geo-politically important, especially since the seventeenth century.

2. Taiwan has been colonized a number of times between the seventeenth and twentieth centuries after the Portuguese sailors discovered Taiwan in the mid-sixteenth century. Taiwan's colonizers included the Dutch, the Spanish, and most recently, the Japanese. This colonial history gave rise to Taiwan's rich and diverse culture as well as to a legal system that is open to the transplantation of foreign laws.

3. The majority of the Chinese in Taiwan are Han Chinese who emigrated from China to Taiwan at different points in time after the seventeenth century. Chinese customary laws, which were largely derived from the agricultural economy of mainland China, played a prominent role especially during the pre-industrialization era, interacting with the Western-centric laws introduced by the colonial powers and, later, by the Taiwanese government after the Second World War.

B. Economy and Law

4. Taiwan was predominantly an agricultural economy until the 1950s, during which time industrialization began. In the later part of the twentieth century, Taiwan went through a period of rapid modernization and industrialization and became an advanced industrial economy. Studies of Taiwan's industrialization and successful economic transition often conclude that Taiwan practiced a form of state capitalism during those years. In contrast, Taiwan's current economy is dynamic and export-driven with the state significantly decreasing its involvement. The agriculture sector only accounts for 1.8% of the GDP, while the industrial sector for 34.8% and the service sector for as much as 63.4%. Accordingly, only 27.6% of the land was considered agricultural land as of 2014, whereas the remainder was designated for mining, industrial, residential, or other urban purposes.[1]

5. A legal system, especially its private laws, reflects the structure of the economy and the society of any given jurisdiction. The characteristics of Taiwan's economy and society explain the dynamics of comprehensive legal reforms in the area of private law. For instance, the transformation from agricultural to industrial economy led to the need for an overhaul of the Taiwan Civil Code among others. The Taiwan Civil Code, similar to those of several other civil-law countries, includes contract, torts, property, family, and inheritance laws. It has gone through a series of comprehensive amendments in 2007, 2009, and 2010. This volume discusses the changes made to the trust and property laws in the following chapters.

II. Cultural Background

6. As an immigrant society, Taiwanese culture is a hybrid of various other cultures. The majority (approximately 97.3%) of Taiwanese are Han Chinese, whereas aborigines are both ethnically and economically in the minority. Various ethnic groups emigrating from different parts of China also brought with them different cultures. Additionally, the colonial powers also imposed their respective cultures and institutions on the Taiwanese people. As a result, Taiwanese culture incorporates traditional Chinese customs, traditional Confucian beliefs, Japanese culture, and, increasingly, Western values.[2]

7. Several features of Taiwanese culture have affected the configurations of its legal system and legal culture, including property law and its enforcement. To begin with, Taiwanese culture per se has given birth to several types of legal rights. *Dian*, an ancient and unique property right which was derived from the Chinese agricultural economy is one case in point. *Dian* allows the landowner to capitalize on the value of agricultural land while preserving the traditional Chinese perspective that land forms a crucial part of a family legacy and should not be treated as a commodity for sale. As a result, *dian* is technically similar to a mortgage but effectively like the transfer of a fee simple.[3]

8. Furthermore, Taiwan's close-knit society (an aspect derived from traditional Chinese culture) can affect the ways in which laws are enforced. Where the cost of enforcing legal rights through the courts, particularly in early years, is higher than

---

1. Data source: Directorate-General of Budget, Accounting and Statistics, Executive Yuan, Taiwan (ROC). http://www.stat.gov.tw/ct.asp?xItem=37407&CtNode=3564&mp=4.
2. Tay-Sheng Wang, *The Legal Development of Taiwan in the 20th Century: Toward a Liberal and Democratic Country*, 11 Pacific Rim & Pol. 531 (2002).
3. For a further discussion, *see* Ch. 1 of Part VI.

§2. LEGAL BACKGROUND OF THE COUNTRY

I. Legal Family or Tradition

14. Taiwan's legal system is based on civil-law tradition introduced through the legal reforms initiated by its own government or its colonizers. The first Western-style court in Taiwan, for example, was created by the Dutch in the seventeenth century. Facing increasing rebellion from the local Taiwanese, the Dutch East India Company aimed to govern Taiwan in a more institutionalized way by creating colonial court in which two appointed Taiwanese representatives jointly oversaw its operations with two Dutch commissioners.[6]

15. Taiwan's legal system has been largely influenced by German and Japanese legal systems.[7] The KMT, while having control over mainland China and before moving to Taiwan, introduced a legal system modeled on that of continental Europe, particularly Germany. When it assumed control of Taiwan in 1945, the KMT did not create a legal system from scratch but simply imported this transplanted legal system that it had established on the mainland. Coincidentally, the Japanese colonial government also introduced a very similar legal system to Taiwan, as its legal system was also modeled on Germany. As a result, two giant waves of early legal transplants in Asia took effect on this island in 1949 when the KMT relocated to Taiwan. This coincidence contributed to the modernization of Taiwan's legal system beginning as early as the late nineteenth century.

16. Specifically, Taiwanese property law is embedded in the Taiwan Civil Code, which was significantly influenced by the German Civil Code and the Swiss Civil Code. In the following decades after its enactment, Taiwanese judges and scholars commonly cited German and Japanese references for the purpose of interpreting similar legal concepts. More recently, the 2009 amendment to the Taiwan Civil Code introduced a new type of mortgage —the line-of-credit mortgage, and this new mortgage was transplanted wholesale from Japanese law.

17. Additionally, Chinese customary law and tradition have remained influential, affecting the formation of legal rights, the interpretation of legal concepts, and their enforcement. During the colonial era, the Japanese government largely accommodated Chinese customary law for practical reasons (e.g., peaceful and efficient governance). In the early twentieth century, the colonial government also comprehensively investigated Chinese customary laws in Taiwan for the purpose of paving the way for Japanese law to be introduced to its colony. When the KMT took over Taiwan after the Second World War, the Taiwanese judiciary continued to reconcile

6. Tay-Sheng Wang, Hua-Yuan Hsueh & Wen-Jie Huang, *Traces of Taiwan Law History* (Wu-Nan Publishing, 2006).
7. For a further discussion on legal transplantation in Taiwan over the past century, *see* Tay-Sheng Wang, *Translation, Codification and Transplantation of Foreign Laws in Taiwan*, 25 Washington Intl. L. J. 307 (2016).

formal law with local customary law except where customary law contradicted public policy and moral principles. Moreover, the Taiwan Civil Code also attempted to codify some widely accepted customary laws, such as "Hui" (or "bid society"), a type of rotating savings and credit cooperatives, which was common and finally formalized by the amendment to the Taiwan Civil Code in 2000.

II. Relation and Hierarchy Between the Sources of Law

18. Taiwan's Constitution took effect in 1946 and has been revised several times in the following decades, especially during the years of democratization. The Constitution widely protects civil, social, and political rights, and such basic rights must not be restricted unless by law subject to the proportionality principle. Article 23 of the Constitution states that "all the freedoms and rights ... shall not be restricted by law except by such as may be necessary to prevent infringement upon the freedoms and rights of other persons, to avert an imminent crisis, to maintain social order, or to advance public welfare." The Constitutional Court, in charge of judicial review and constitutional interpretations, is a standalone institution independent of the three-level ordinary court system.

19. The Legislative Yuan is the central government's sole law-making body. In addition to general legislative power, it is also delegated the power to initiate proposals for amending the Constitution subject to ratification by popular referendum. The Referendum Act was enacted in 2004 for exercising the right of direct democracy stipulated in the Constitution.[8]

20. A statute promulgated by the Legislative Yuan may be named as an act, a penal act,[9] a special act, or a comprehensive act. An "act" is most often used to designate general provisions of law. A "special act" is usually reserved for statutes of a narrower and more specific ambit. In comparison, the government agencies of the Executive Yuan can enact ordinances pursuant to their inherent or delegated powers so long as these ordinances do not contradict the Constitution and laws.[10]

21. Precedents in Taiwan operate differently from that of common-law jurisdictions. Taiwan does not have the *stare decisis* doctrine in a strict sense. According to Article 80 of the Constitution, judges must rule independently in accordance with law, not precedents. Therefore, precedents do not bind individual judges. In the past, the Supreme Court selected some of its decisions to be demarcated as "precedents" to ensure the consistent interpretations of certain abstract legal concepts. As a result,

8. The Constitution of the Republic of China (Taiwan), Art. 136.
9. There is no legislation designated as a penal act at present.
10. Zhongyang Fagui Biaozhun Fa [Standard Act for Law and Rules], Arts. 2 and 3.

these selected precedents bound the judges of lower courts de facto[11] Now, according to Article 57-1 of the Court Organization Act, Supreme Court judgments delivered prior to December 7, 2018 and administratively selected as "precedents", from then on should either be suspended (if the facts of the judgments are not available) or have the same effect as Supreme Court judgments that had not been administratively selected as "precedents." The Supreme Court will no longer select judgments as "precedents."

22. The Taiwan Supreme Court itself consists of nine civil divisions, and it is not infrequent that the divisions render opposing decisions. Cases are randomly assigned to the nine civil divisions; thus, no division has a particularly strong influence over, for example, property or trust law. The Taiwan Supreme Court used to employ a system of Civil Division Meeting Resolution; in essence, this used to consist of an informal *en banc* meeting of all the Supreme Court judges who would debate and use majority voting to resolve split jurisprudence of the Taiwan Supreme Court.[12] Judges at the level of the Taiwan Supreme Court, as well as judges in lower courts, would generally attach significant weight to a Civil Division Meeting Resolution. However, it was not unheard of for judges in one or more of the nine civil divisions of the Taiwan Supreme Court to continue to apply a viewpoint different from one that had been articulated in a Civil Division Meeting Resolution. This was possible because a Civil Division Meeting Resolution was not legally binding. New jurisprudence would be developed to avoid the unequitable outcomes resulting from strictly adhering to the resolutions.

23. On July 4, 2019, the system of Civil Division Meeting Resolutions (also called Resolution by the En Banc Conference of the Civil Tribunal) was abolished and the new Grand Chamber system of the Supreme Court was launched. Preexisting Civil Division Meeting Resolutions now merely have the status of legal opinions that had been expressed by some Supreme Court judges outside the adjudication context.

III. Civil Procedure System

24. There are three types of court procedures: small-claim procedure, summary procedure, and ordinary procedure. The small-claim procedure applies when the amount at stake is below 100,000 NTD (approximately 3,300 USD). Small-claim

11. The de facto binding effect of precedents has resulted in many debates among scholars as to how to deal with unconstitutional precedents. In the controversial Interpretation No. 154 (1978) of the Constitutional Court, the Grand Justices said that "the legal precedents of the Supreme Court and Administrative Court shall have binding effect and can be the bases for courts at all levels in rendering their respective judgments … [T]he Grand Justices Council Adjudication Act is applicable if and when the issue of constitutionality is present so that the rights of the people can be maintained." This interpretation is controversial, as it raised the position of precedents in the hierarchy of law to a level similar to law even though precedents do not have such a status in Taiwan.
12. The resolutions typically contain a legal question with minimal, stripped down fact patterns, a number of competing legal arguments, and a conclusion based on votes.

cases are handled by a single judge in one of the 22 district courts. A case applying ordinary procedure is handled by a single judge in the district court. Appeals are handled by a three-judge panel in one of the six high courts. The review of facts and laws is *de novo*. Cases with more than 1,500,000 NTD (approximately 50,000 USD) at stake may be appealed to the Taiwan Supreme Court on questions of law.

§3. Introduction to the Law of Property and Trust

I. Historical Origins and Evolution

A. *Enactment in 1929*

25. The original Taiwan Civil Code was enacted in 1929 and went into force in 1930 when the Nationalist Government still ruled China.[13] Since 1949, the Civil Code has been the private law of the land in Taiwan. The 1929 Civil Code was drafted with the assistance of Japanese consultants and was heavily influenced by German Civil Code and Swiss Civil Code. That said, both the original and the amended Book of Things in the Taiwan Civil Code are far from carbon copies of the German, Swiss, or the Japanese Civil Code. The Japanese Civil Code treats possession as a right and contains comprehensive stipulations regarding priority rights (other than mortgage and pledge), while the Taiwan Civil Code conceptualizes possession as a fact and does not have any priority right other than mortgage and pledge. In Japan and Taiwan, land and buildings are separate real estates, while under the German Civil Code, a building is generally part of a land parcel. The drafters of the Taiwan Civil Code incorporated the "*dian* right," a traditional Chinese property right absent in Germany, Switzerland, and Japan, while leaving out certain use rights (such as *usufruct*) and security rights (such as land charges) that were both adopted in the German Civil Code but were distant from property practice in China.

26. After decades of application in Taiwan, loopholes, big and small, emerged. The Taiwan Supreme Court, through its selected "precedent" system, filled in the holes while sometimes creating other problems. As noted above, this selected "precedent" system has been abolished. After two failed attempts to change the Book of Things in the Taiwan Civil Code, the Taiwan Civil Code eventually went through a major overhaul in 2007–2010.

B. *Amendment in 2007–2010*

27. The Ministry of Justice is in charge of the enactment and revision of many laws in Taiwan, including the Taiwan Civil Code. In 1988, the Ministry of Justice

13. This section is adapted from Yun-chien Chang, *The Evolution of Property Law in Taiwan: An Unconventional Interest Group Story, in Private Law in China and Taiwan: Economic and Legal Analyses* 212 (Yun-chien Chang et al. eds, 2016).

organized a task force composed of judges and legal scholars to draft the proposed revisions of the Book of Things in the Taiwan Civil Code. After 300 meetings over eight years, the bill was sent to the legislature but was not passed. In 2003, the Ministry of Justice organized another task force to improve the bill. The revised bill was divided into three parts and sent out to the legislature separately. In 2007, 2009, and 2010, the legislature passed the part on securities, the parts on general principle and ownership, and the parts on use rights and possession, respectively. Before 2007, there were 210 articles in the Book of Things and only one of them had been revised since its enactment in 1929 in China.[14]

28. Many laws in Taiwan were revised upon suggestions by the Executive Yuan (the cabinet) or the Judicial Yuan (responsible for supervising judges, etc.). Either Yuan typically sends to the legislature a document starting with an executive summary, followed by a table that contains three columns: the current statutes, the proposed revisions, and the "underlying reasons" for amendment, article by article. That is, each amended article is accompanied by its own underlying reason. These "underlying reasons" are not official (i.e., the legislature does not *pass* these reasons), but they are good sources for probing into the driving forces of legal changes.

29. On the basis of the number of citations to foreign laws in the "underlying reasons," the Japanese Civil Code may be the most influential foreign civil code in Taiwan. But the citation number over-states its influence, as a lot of references concern the new property form—line-of-credit mortgage—that the Taiwan Civil Code imported from the Japanese Civil Code wholesale. The original Taiwan Civil Code was heavily influenced by German and Swiss Civil Codes, so their continued influence is not surprising—references to German Civil Code concentrate on stipulations regarding ownership and general principle.

II. The Concept of Ownership

A. Unity and Fragmentation

30. Due to the continuous German and Swiss influence on the Taiwan Civil Code, the mainstream conception of ownership is still German. In other words, ownership is considered as a unity, only burdened by various limited property rights. The "bundle-of-rights" analogy popular in the U.S. is rarely drawn upon by scholars.

14. Taiwan Civil Code, Art. 942 was revised in 1995 to correct a typo.

B. Immovable and Real Property (See Also Part I)

31. The Taiwan Civil Code distinguishes between immovable and movable properties. Immovables are land and buildings.[15] Movables are things other than immovable properties.[16] Things under the Taiwan Civil Code are mostly corporeal—the pledge over rights is the only exception, as objects of this property right are claims rather than corporeal things. Chose in action, intellectual property rights, funds, etc., are not considered movable properties.

32. Land and buildings (and completed construction works) are separate things. A person owning a house and the underlying land would own at least two property rights: one for the house and the other for the land parcel. Very often, the house and the underlying land are owned by different persons. This is why *superficies* is very important in Taiwan. Also note that Constitutional Interpretation No. 93 declares that light rails, unless temporary in nature, are construction works. Zui Gao Fa Yuan [Taiwanese Supreme Court] 6th Civil Resolution Meeting of Year 1974 declares that buildings and construction works become stand-alone real properties when they shield rains and wind and can be used economically.

C. Movable and Personal Property (See Also Part II)

33. Movables are corporeal things that are not immovable.

III. Estate and Patrimony

34. Almost no succession-law scholars and no court opinions recognize the concept of estate, although it could be quite useful.[17] In the realm of property law, Taiwan as a civil-law jurisdiction does not formally recognize the notion of estate, and no future interests are recognized in Book III of the Taiwan Civil Code.

35. The concept of patrimony is only gradually entering the legal dictionary in Taiwan. Trust fund, partnership asset, etc., are explained by drawing on the German concept *Sondervermögen* (special asset). According to this theory, a person can have one or several *Sondervermögen*, in addition to his or her main asset, as long as a statute explicitly recognizes creating such a special asset. *Sondervermögen* is functionally close to patrimony.[18]

15. Taiwan Civil Code, Art. 66.
16. Taiwan Civil Code, Art. 67.
17. *See* Yun-chien Chang & Sieh-chuen Huang, *Reconceptualizing Estate and Protecting Creditors: Theory and Reform Proposals*, 110 Taipei U. L. Rev. 171 (2019) [in Chinese].
18. *See* Yun-chien Chang, *Separate Patrimony and Asset Partitioning: A Theoretical Framework*, 50 Cross-Strait L. Rev. 87 (2015) [in Chinese].

IV. Possession and Title

36. Possession and ownership are distinct concepts.[19] Ownership is a full right to real or personal properties while possession, defined as actual control, is a fact.[20] They each have a chapter of their own in Book III of the Taiwan Civil Code. The ownership chapter runs from Articles 765–831. The possession chapter, the last one in Book III, runs from Articles 940–966. "Possession is 9/10 of the law" is not a Taiwan Civil Code doctrine. Possession of immovable properties leads to titles only through acquisitive prescription,[21] which is bordering on impossible nowadays. Possessors of unregistered immovables (mostly illegal buildings) and movables are presumed to have a legitimate right.[22]

---

19. Norman Barry observes that "in civil law, there is an attempt to distinguish *ownership* from *possession*, which is not a crucial feature of common law" (emphasis original) and that "common law does not make a great deal of difference between possession and ownership; they are treated as much the same. But in civil law, ownership is very important, and a code's emphasis on it has prevented efficient property rights from developing." Norman Barry, *Property Rights in Common and Civil Law, in The Elgar Companion to the Economics of Property Rights* 180, 184 (Enrico Colombatto ed., Edward Elgar 2004).
20. More discussion, *see* Yun-chien Chang, *The Economy of Concept and Possession, in Law and Economics of Possession* 103 (Yun-chien Chang ed., Cambridge Univ. Press 2015).
21. Yun-chien Chang, *Adverse Possession Laws in 203 Jurisdictions: Proposals for Reform,* 43 U. PA. J. INT'L L. 373 (2022).
22. Taiwan Civil Code, Art. 943.

Part I. Immovable Property and Real Property

Chapter 1. General Classification

§1. Land and Buildings (and Other Construction Works) as Separate Real Properties

37. In Taiwan, buildings and construction works on land are not considered to be a part of land. The ownership of land and the ownership of buildings on such land are separate objects for the purposes of demarcating property rights, although both are considered real properties under Taiwan's property law regime.

38. While both types of ownership are treated equally as rights in rem in immovable properties, the formalities needed to create such a right in rem are slightly different than common-law jurisdictions. Like Australia, Singapore, and several other jurisdictions, Taiwan has adopted the Torrens registration-of-right system to register real rights in land. Under the Torrens system, the creation, transfer and, alteration of property rights will not take effect without registration. Put differently, registration of real rights is constitutive. Registration, however, is optional for real rights related to buildings, construction works, and other fixtures. Such a distinction has caused tremendous problems in practice with respect to illegal buildings, which have not been brought under the Torrens system in Taiwan but have been, for all practical purposes, transacted and transferred in informal markets.[23]

23. These buildings, built by owners or developers who have failed to comply with the relevant building ordinances, have been transacted in informal markets. The Supreme Court once acknowledged that the owners of these illegal buildings have "rights of *de facto* disposal" for practical reasons. The tax agency also put them in the tax registry in order to levy property tax. All such practical measures have further complicated the issues surrounding such informal property rights. *See* Yun-chien Chang & Henry E. Smith, *The Numerus Clausus Principle, Property Customs, and the Emergence of New Property Forms*, 100 Iowa L. R. 2275 (2015).

§2. PRIVATE VERSUS PUBLIC OWNERSHIP

39. In Taiwan, private and public ownership of immovable properties are clearly separate rights. While individuals can own private land and buildings, the governments of all levels may also own state land and buildings pursuant to relevant laws and regulations. Generally speaking, each owner, private or public, has absolute control over the property owned.

40. This principle is in line with the conception of property ownership pursuant to civil-law tradition. In terms of land ownership, civil-law tradition emphasizes "dominium," or the absolute and direct ownership of the land, which is derived from Roman law. This is in contrast to common-law property, under which land is all owned by the state or the Crown. Accordingly, the state or the Crown rely on the device of "estates" in land to transact and transfer property interests in land. "Estates" are the proprietary interests carved out from the nominal ownership of land owned by the state or the Crown.[24]

41. Under Taiwan's property law regime, the owner enjoys absolute control and exclusive rights over his immovable property. Article 765 of the Taiwan Civil Code provides that "the property owner has the right, subject to the limits set by other laws and regulations, to use his property, to profit from it, and to dispose of it freely, and to exclude the interference from others." Such private property rights are protected by the Constitution and are not to be restricted except by law as may be necessary to prevent infringement upon the freedoms and rights of other persons, to avert an imminent crisis, to maintain social order, or to advance public welfare.[25] In comparison, greater restrictions are imposed on state land. Examples of such restrictions include the Act for State-owned Assets,[26] Act for National Land Use Planning,[27] and other administrative laws and regulations. For instance, the Act for State-owned Assets provides statutory covenants for leases on state-owned land and stipulates management methods as well as allocation and audit of benefits (e.g., rental income) derived from state-owned land. The Act for National Land Use Planning provides a holistic assessment and regulatory framework for nationwide land use, especially for the purpose of conservation and environmental protection in order to reverse the trend of excessive development in some parts of the country over the decades.

24. *See* Yun-chien Chang & Henry E. Smith, *An Economic Analysis of Civil Versus Common Law Property*, 88 NOTRE DAME L. REV. 1 (2012).
25. The Constitution of the Republic of China (Taiwan), Art. 23.
26. Guoyou Caichan Fa [The Act for State-owned Assets] (1969).
27. Guotu Jihua Fa [The Act for National Land Use Planning] (2016).

Chapter 2. Legal Interests

§1. Ownership

42. In Taiwan, private ownership of land and buildings is the norm.

43. "The owner of a thing has the right, within the limits of law, to use it, to profit from it, to dispose of it freely, and to exclude the interference from others."[28] Owners' rights to exclude lead to the revindication right (*rei vindicatio*). More specifically, "the owner of a thing has the right to demand its return from anyone, who possesses it without authority or who seizes it. Where his ownership is interfered, he is entitled to claim the removal of the interference; and where the ownership might be interfered, he is entitled to an injunction to prevent such interference."[29]

44. The Taiwan Civil Code further limits the landowners' right to exclude. The Taiwan Civil Code Article 773 starts with a limited endorsement of the *ad coelum* rule by stipulating that "unless otherwise restricted by law, ownership of land extends to above and below the surface of the land, to the extent it benefits the owner." Then, the Taiwan Civil Code Article 773 restricts landowners' right to exclude—"Interference from others shall not be excluded if it does not obstruct the exercise of the ownership." Note that the Taiwan Civil Code Article 773 only applies to land; buildings and other construction works are not included.

45. The relationship between ownership and possession is explained in more detail in the Introduction and Chapter 3 of Part III. Stipulations regarding neighbor relations,[30] including condominium law,[31] are covered in Chapter 7 of Part I.

§2. Registration

46. Taiwan, like Germany, adopts the Torrens registration system.[32] Land registration is mandatory and the Department of Land Administration, Ministry of the Interior, has actively mapped land in Taiwan and put it in the registry. More than 97% of land in Taiwan has been mapped and registered. Most of the unregistered land is state land exempted by the Land Act for registration purposes.

---

28. Taiwan Civil Code, Art. 765.
29. Taiwan Civil Code, Art. 767.
30. Taiwan Civil Code, Arts. 774–800.
31. *See* Yun-chien Chang, *Condominium Law in Taiwan: Doctrinal Overview under the Lens of Information-Cost Theory*, 23 Asia Pac. L. Rev. 89 (2015).
32. For a cliometric study that shows that introducing land registration in Taiwan under Japanese rule in the early twentieth century had increased legal certainty to title and thus increased farmers' long-term investment, *see* Hui-Wen Koo, *Property Rights, Land Prices, and Investment: A Study of the Taiwanese Land Registration System*, 167 JITE 515 (2011).

47. Registration of buildings and construction works is optional. Builders of their own houses, for example, can choose to leave their constructions off the registry, at the expense of not being able to transfer ownership or establish limited property rights de jure. Many developers do not register buildings, however, because they have failed to comply with the building code—that is, they cannot register even if they want to. (The tax authorities seek out these buildings and construction works and put them in the tax registry to levy property taxes anyway.) These kinds of buildings and construction works, called "illegal buildings" in Taiwan, cause courts in Taiwan a lot of trouble: numerous illegal buildings exist and were exchanged, and yet, legally speaking, no formal property rights changed hands. In the late 1950s, the Taiwan Supreme Court was forced to create a new type of property right, called the "right of *de facto* disposal." More on this in Chapter 3 of Part I.

48. Legal transfers of real property rights are not effective before registration in the land registry; the registration application has to be in writing.[33] Nonetheless, a person who has acquired property rights by succession, court enforcement, expropriation, a court verdict, or other non-juridical acts becomes the legal owner before registration but can convey property rights only after registering the property.[34]

49. Registration gives notice to the public. Right holders recorded in the registry are thus presumed to hold the rights legitimately.[35] Moreover, good-faith third parties who rely on the registered information in their conveyance of real rights will be protected even when the registered information is incorrect.[36] This is called the "public faith principle" or absolutism in real property registration.

---

33. Taiwan Civil Code, Art. 758.
34. Taiwan Civil Code, Art. 759.
35. Taiwan Civil Code, Art. 759-1.
36. Taiwan Civil Code, Art. 759-1.

Chapter 3. Equitable Interests

50. There is no such thing as an equitable interest under the Taiwan Civil Code. This chapter is instead used to introduce the customary property rights, which are conceptually close to equitable interests in the common law.

§1. The Numerus Clausus Principle

I. Legislative Stipulation and Judicial Application

51. The *numerus clausus* principle means that the legislature monopolizes the creation of property forms. This principle was promulgated in the first article of Book III of the Taiwan Civil Code in 1929.[37] German jurisprudence usefully categorizes this principle into two elements: the fixed content of property forms (*Typenfixierung*) and the limited number of types of property forms (*Typenzwang*). Under this principle, a contract that aims to have third-party (or, in rem) effect without conforming to any of the statute-prescribed forms would either be considered invalid or only effective between the contracting parties.

52. In 2009, Taiwan moved from the strict *numerus clausus* principle to a system under which both statutes and customary laws can create property forms.[38]
As of June 2021, courts in Taiwan have not formally recognized customary property forms, although they have done so implicitly (*see* Chapter 3, §2).

II. Types of Limited Property Rights in Taiwan Civil Code

53. Owing to the *numerus clausus* principle, the several types of property forms (limited property rights) sanctioned by the Taiwan Civil Code and other statutes are the only choices for transacting parties who prefer a deal with in rem effects.[39] Property rights delineated by the Taiwan Civil Code are briefly introduced below and explained in more detail in Part II and Part III.

A. *Use Rights*

54. The Taiwan Civil Code acknowledges three types of "use rights" (*Nutzungsrecht* in German): *superficies*, real easement (easement appurtenant), and agricultural right. *Emphyteusis*, or permanent tenancy rights, a traditional form dating back to Roman law but rarely utilized nowadays (less than fifty new creations each

37. Taiwan Civil Code, Art. 757.
38. Taiwan Civil Code, Art. 757.
39. This section is adapted from Yun-chien Chang, *The Evolution of Property Law in Taiwan: An Unconventional Interest Group Story*, in *Private Law in China and Taiwan: Economic and Legal Analyses* (Yun-chien Chang et al. eds., Cambridge Univ. Press 2016).

year)[40] was abolished in 2010 and replaced by a new agricultural right. As noted above, land and buildings are separate real estates, which make *superficies*, or above-ground rights,[41] a crucial right in land use planning. Only *superficies* enables owners of buildings or construction works to legally use the land underneath their building without interruption by landowners before the *superficies* expires. When contracting over temporary immovable property uses, many property owners still use leases, a type of contract with only *in personam* effect, resulting in lawsuits and disputes regarding building demolition,[42] while owners of such buildings do not have the right to use the underlying land.

55. Before 2010, real easements (or servitudes) could only be set between two land parcels. Now they can be set between any real properties, such as between a house and a land parcel. Only easements appurtenant, but not easements in gross, are allowed. Non-compete easement never took off in Taiwan; even passage easements are uncommon. The amended Taiwan Civil Code[43] and the Condominium Administration Act enable developers and residents to use covenants running with real properties in planning and managing condominium or large-scale neighborhoods. Doctrinally, this is a breakthrough, but the market has not picked up this tool.

B. Security Rights

56. The current Taiwan Civil Code specifies three types of securities rights:[44] mortgage, pledge, and lien. Mortgage (called *hypothec* in European civil-law countries, and *Diya* in Chinese) is by far the most popular limited property right in Taiwan, with hundreds of thousands of registrations filed to create new mortgages each year.

57. The 2009 amendment of the Taiwan Civil Code formally introduced a subtype of mortgage into the code, line-of-credit mortgage. Despite the strict *numerus clausus* principle in the original Taiwan Civil Code, courts and banks since the 1960s have recognized this form of mortgage, which softens the accessory principle, allowing both parties to stipulate the maximum amount of credit in the loan contract without requiring the lender to borrow out the full amount at the outset. Business lending often takes this form. By contrast, home mortgage is always in the

40. The demise of *emphyteusis* should be attributed to the large-scale land reform in the 1950s, during which the land use laws stipulated that tenants received ownership—through eminent domain—after twenty years of leasing. Permanent tenants, as a result, essentially disappeared.
41. Above-ground rights are a literal translation. *Superficies* can in fact be established for developments below land surface. *See* Art. 832 of the Taiwanese Civil Code.
42. This led to the enactment of Arts. 425-1 and 426-1 of the Taiwan Civil Code.
43. Taiwan Civil Code, Arts. 799-1, 859-4.
44. Unlike many other civil law countries, the Taiwanese Civil Code explicitly treats security rights as types of property forms, rather than contractual forms or intermediate forms. Yun-chien Chang & Henry E. Smith, *Structure and Style in Comparative Property Law, in Research Handbook on Comparative Law and Economics* (Giovannia B. Ramello & Theodore Eisenberg eds., Edward Elgar 2016).

form of a traditional mortgage. Home mortgage loans were heavily regulated even before the 2008 U.S. Financial Crisis. As such, home mortgage payments are generally amortized.

C. Dian, a Hybrid Form

58. A hybrid form, *dian* right is analogous to but still different from *anticresis* (or *antichresis* or usufructuary mortgage) under which a creditor collects natural and/or legal yields which are used to offset interest on debt. *Anticresis* is distinguished from *dian* in their attitudes toward the foreclosure clause. If a foreclosure clause is allowed, parties can specify in advance that if debtors default, their creditors acquire ownership of the collateral. By contrast, under *dian*, interests, but not principals, are presumed to perfectly cancel out the proceeds during the *dian* relationship, and the foreclosure clause is perhaps the whole point of *dian*. In a *dian* arrangement, a landowner sells ownership to a purchaser with an *in rem* buy-back option to be exercised within multiple decades (according to Civil Code of Taiwan (TCC) Article 912, thirty years is the maximal period that a *dian* can last), but historically a *dian* could last more than a century. The option strike price is the original *dian* price (TCC Article 924). *Dian* rights are even more unpopular than the permanent tenancy right and were rarely used in the past several decades. Yet, the legislature preserved this form and greatly amended the relevant stipulations in the Taiwan Civil Code, hoping to rekindle interest in *dian* right.[45] *Dian* right can be traced back to the Song Dynasty in China (about 1000 years ago) and was quite popular in Taiwan until 1923 (the later stage of Japanese colonization), when the Japanese government mandated conformation with the Japanese Civil Code, which did not recognize *dian* right. *Dian* is similar to but not the same as *anticresis*.

§2. CUSTOMARY PROPERTY RIGHTS IN ACTION

59. Despite the strict *numerus clausus* principle that was in force before 2009, all levels of courts in Taiwan have allowed for at least three types of limited property rights that were not recognized by any statute—thus violating the *numerus clausus* principle.[46] More specifically, they are the line-of-credit mortgage, commercial pledge of personal property, and right of de facto disposal on illegal buildings. In 2020, the Supreme Court of Taiwan, for the first time, explicitly recognized "ownership assigned as collateral" as a form of customary property right.

---

45. Tsay-chuan Hsieh, *The Amendment of the Book of Things in the Taiwanese Civil Code*, 100 TAIWAN L. R. 27 (2007) [in Chinese].
46. This section is adapted from Yun-chien Chang & Henry E. Smith, *The Numerus Clausus Principle, Property Custom, and the Emergence of New Property Forms*, 100 Iowa L. R. 2275 (2015).

I. Line-of-Credit Mortgage and Commercial Pledges of Personal Property

60. The line-of-credit mortgage is a recognized customary property form in Japan[47] and was imported to Taiwan in the early twentieth century when Taiwan was under Japanese rule from 1895 to 1945. The line-of-credit mortgage was widely used after 1945 in the market as an ordinary mortgage plus a new type of security contract. Then the Ministry of Finance requested all banks to take line-of-credit mortgages. At the same time, local land registrars were also mandated to accept registrations of line-of-credit mortgages. In addition, the Ministry of Justice—in the old days of the authoritarian regime—requested that the district courts and appellate courts stand out of the way. The line-of-credit mortgage thus became a recognized property form, albeit customary. The line-of-credit mortgage had been and still is a heavily used form of security interest.

61. Another example is the commercial pledge of personal property (pawn), which was approved by the Taiwan Supreme Court, probably because of the following reasons: the civil code recognizes the noncommercial pledge as a property form in the civil code; an administrative rule (not a statute) lays out the contours of the right; pawning is very common; and pawn shops are heavily regulated.

62. In the 2007 amendment of the Taiwan Civil Code, the legislature has formally incorporated the commercial pledge of personal property[48] and the line-of-credit mortgage[49] into the Taiwan Civil Code. Thus, these two customary rights have now been elevated to formal property rights.

II. Right of De Facto Disposal and Illegal Buildings

63. Starting from the 1950s, many buildings in Taiwan were constructed without permits and thus could not be registered in the official real estate registry. Under the Taiwan Civil Code,[50] however, ownership and other real rights can be de jure transferred only if they are registered.[51] These "illegal buildings" have been traded anyway, and in large volumes. Courts could have ruled that no property rights had been legally transferred; instead, through a series of precedents, the Supreme Court

47. The line-of-credit mortgage was incorporated into the Japanese Civil Code in 1971.
48. The Legislative Yuan of Taiwan also enacted the Pawnshop Act in 2010. *See* Taiwan Civil Code, Art. 899-2.
49. Taiwan Civil Code, Arts. 881-1 to 881-17.
50. Taiwan Civil Code, Art. 758.
51. More exactly, the precondition for registering such transfers, in the case of buildings or construction works, is that they have undergone "the initial registration of ownership." Since the 1960s, however, only developers (or owners) of buildings or construction works with proper building permits in compliance with all the building code regulations are allowed to file for the initial registration. That is, while the underlying land parcels could have been registered, the buildings upon them may never be registered.

in Taiwan has repeatedly held that although ownership did not change hands, the buyers acquired a "right of *de facto* disposal," which, of course, is nonexistent in the civil code.

64. One may expect that the law thus discouraged developers from building illegally. While it might have prevented some rational and risk-averse people from the illegal business, many were not deterred. Indeed, a market for illegal buildings has been in place for half a century. Illegal buildings are so prevalent that even the Constitutional Court of Taiwan has its office in one!

65. The Taiwanese executive branch is not very active in solving the illegal building problem. This is perhaps because it is too big of a problem and a strong-arm policy may win elected officials a small gain in popularity at the expense of the votes of holders of de facto disposal rights. The administrative agencies instead pursue a four-fold strategy: (1) the registrar denies registration; (2) the enforcement department tears down a small percentage of illegal buildings that its budget and manpower allow it to do; (3) the tax authority levies property tax on illegal buildings (though the tax rates for legal and illegal buildings are the same); and (4) at most one-time, small-amount civil fines are imposed.

66. Lawsuits flooded the courts. From the get-go, the Taiwan Supreme Court did not take the position that illegal buildings are inalienable (which would be consistent with the Taiwan Civil Code). Thus, the Taiwan Supreme Court had to offer an explanation as to what kind of right changes hands and through which notice mechanism. Doctrinally, the illegal and unregistered buildings are hard to classify. Buildings are immovables, so the delivery-and-transfer rule for movable properties does not apply. Illegal buildings are, if anything, real properties, but the registration policy shuts the door to their legal transactions. Thus, finding a route to legal enforceability is no easy task.

67. To make a long story short, the Taiwan Supreme Court in 1952 ruled that developers gained ownership through original acquisition (i.e., by building the buildings or construction works)[52] and that developers, as owners of illegal buildings, could not transfer ownership or any limited property right to others.[53] Nonetheless, they could sell the "right of *de facto* disposal," which is roughly coterminous with the right to destroy. The right was named as such because it was originally conceptualized to deal with the question of whether a buyer of illegal buildings may tear it down and not be obliged to pay the "owner" damages. Since the 1960s, the Taiwan Supreme Court, through a series of decisions and precedents,[54] gradually clarified and enriched the content of the right of de facto disposal—but note that the Taiwan Supreme Court never explicitly required any

52. Zui Gao Fa Yuan 41 Nian Tai Shang Zi Di 1039 Hao Pan Li [Supreme Court 1952 No. 1039 Precedent].
53. Zui Gao Fa Yuan [Supreme Court] 2nd Civil Resolution Meeting of Year 1978.
54. *See, e.g.*, Zui Gao Fa Yuan 52 Nian Tai Shang Zi Di 681 Hao Pan Li [Supreme Court 1963 No. 681 Precedent]; Zui Gao Fa Yuan 48 Nian Tai Shang Zi Di 1812 Hao Pan Li [Supreme Court 1959 No.

notice mechanism, not even a change of possession. Now the right includes various use rights but the original name sticks. Basically, buyers of illegal buildings (or holders of rights of de facto disposal) can use and enjoy the building very much in the same way owners do,[55] but banks have been reluctant to accept illegal buildings as security.

68. The right of de facto disposal has fuzzy edges, however. Because of the stringent *numerus clausus* principle in the Taiwan Civil Code when the Supreme Court shaped this new right, the Supreme Court never spelled out whether the right of de facto disposal is a contractual right or a property right. This ambiguity confuses everyone involved, including the courts themselves.[56] Consider this example: A constructs an illegal house and then sells it to B, and B then sells it to C. When C possesses the house, A goes bankrupt. A's creditor forecloses on the house in question and petitions the court to auction the house to pay off A's debt.[57] According to Taiwanese law, only parties with a property interest can object and stop the auction proceedings. C's right of de facto disposal is not considered a property right for this purpose under the Supreme Court's jurisprudence. Thus, C is unable to stop A's or B's creditors from foreclosing his or her house. A lot of people in the situation of C have brought lawsuits, hoping to sway the court to alter this unreasonable ruling, but so far to no avail.

69. It is understandable that before the 2009 amendment of the Taiwan Civil Code, the Taiwan Supreme Court was reluctant to disregard the civil code and to declare that the right of de facto disposal is a full-fledged property right. After 2009, the Taiwan Supreme Court finally has the power to clarify the nature of right of de facto disposal. What will the Taiwan Supreme Court do? Stay tuned. As of June 2021, the Taiwan Supreme Court has not clarified the nature of the right of de facto disposal.

III. Ownership Assigned as Collateral

70. In a 2020 case, the Supreme Court of Taiwan recognized that "ownership assigned as collateral" is a form of customary property right.[58] "Ownership assigned as collateral" is the literal translation of the term used in Chinese (*rangyu danbao*). Under the title theory of mortgage, it could be thought of as a mortgage—but it is

---

1812 Precedent]; Zui Gao Fa Yuan 50 Nian Tai Shang Zi Di 1236 Hao Pan Li [Supreme Court 1961 No. 1236 Precedent]; Zui Gao Fa Yuan 69 Nian Tai Shang Zi Di 3726 Hao Pan Li [Supreme Court 1980 No. 3726 Precedent].

55. Thus, one may contend that the right of de facto disposal is functionally ownership. Nonetheless, doctrinally speaking, the right of de facto disposal would have to count as a new form.
56. Sometimes courts treat the right of de facto disposal as a contractual right, sometimes a property right.
57. If B goes bankrupt and B's creditor files for foreclosure and auction, courts would rule in the same way.
58. Zui Gao Fa Yuan 109 Nian Tai Shang Zi Di 3214 Hao Pan Jue [Supreme Court 2020 No. 3214 Judgment].

different from the *diya* (Taiwan Civil Code Article 860), which is translated by the Ministry of Justice as mortgage.[59] Before 1996, when the Trust Act was enacted, "ownership assigned as collateral" was often described by the Supreme Court as "ownership assigned in trust as collateral." "Ownership assigned as collateral" can be exemplified by the facts in two Supreme Court cases. In Supreme Court 1991 No. 1813 Judgment and Supreme Court 1991 No. 2565 Judgment, A registered her premises under B's name as collateral to B for A's debt. In both cases, the legal effect of so-called "ownership assigned in trust as collateral" was described as follows: (1) if A paid his debt before the due date, B had to register the premises back to A's name; but (2) if A defaulted, B could sell the collateral and collect the debt from the proceeds. The creditor in this type of case, therefore, has a power of disposition which is conditional on the debtor defaulting.[60] "Ownership assigned as collateral" is not a trust as defined by the Trust Act, as the creditor is both the trustee and the sole beneficiary. This violates Article 34 of the Trust Act, which provides that a trustee cannot be the sole beneficiary ("A trustee shall on no account be entitled to any benefits arising out of a trust unless the trustee is a co-beneficiary of the trust."). Supreme Court 2020 No. 3214 Judgment explicitly rules that "ownership assigned as collateral" is not a type of trust, as it violates Article 34 of the Trust Act. Thus, it can be implied that "ownership assigned as collateral" is a new type of property right, but not a new type of trust form.

§3. Property Right System of the Aboriginal People

71. Indigenous people in Taiwan traditionally have a different conception of property rights, and the new Taiwan Civil Code Article 757 opens the door to them to keep their traditional property system. Scholars have put in efforts to systematize the property theories of the several tribes of aboriginal people in Taiwan, hoping to provide courts with anthropologically informed legal discourses. Progress has been made, but as of June 2021, courts in Taiwan have not recognized a single customary property right based on aboriginal customs.

59. The mortgage as such adopts the lien theory of mortgage. A less confusing translation would be *hypothec* or charge. But this book follows the Ministry of Justice translation and the IEL guideline in calling *diya* mortgage.
60. For an overview of "ownership assigned in trust as collateral", *see* Tsay-chuan Hsieh, *The Evolution of Case Law: "Ownership Assigned as Collateral" as an Example*, 310 Taiwan L. Rev. 178 (2021) [in Chinese].

Chapter 4. Limited Interests

72. Although this chapter is entitled "Limited Interests" to be in line with the shared structure of the book series, we use the term "limited property rights" hereinafter as it better coveys this concept under Taiwan's civil-law tradition.

§1. Usufruct

I. General Conception

73. *Usufruct* carries varying configurations in different jurisdictions. The Taiwan Civil Code does not recognize *usufruct* as the civil code in France does.

74. Instead, the Taiwan Civil Code recognizes three other types of use rights: *superficies*, agricultural rights, and real easements. Specifically, *superficies* and agricultural rights involve the transfer of possession of property for the purpose of utilizing the property entirely, whereas easements are created for a more specific use of a certain part of the servient property for the benefit of the designated dominant tenement. Notably, the Taiwan Civil Code only provides for easement appurtenant but not easement in gross.

75. Prior to the amendment of 2010, there existed another type of use right—*emphyteusis*, or permanent tenancy rights. *Emphyteusis*, a form of property right deriving from Roman law, was rarely utilized in Taiwan and hence was replaced with agricultural rights. Agricultural rights share some basic characteristics with *emphyteusis* but have been modified to suit the need of modern economy and business transactions. This chapter further discusses agricultural rights in the next section.

II. Formality Requirement

76. The statutory formality for creating the types of use rights is provided by Taiwan's Torrens system. Any acquisition, creation, or alternation of property rights has to be made in writing and will not take effect without registration.[61] Article 43 of the Land Act also confirms the indefeasibility of registered titles by stating that "the registration of land title is absolute." Any bona fide successor without notice, who has registered the property in question, shall not be affected and his property rights shall not be vitiated by any defective property and contractual relationships caused or associated with his predecessor(s).[62] The Torrens system facilitates the transactions of property rights by giving such indefeasibility that allows bona fide third parties to engage in market transactions with certainty. That said, similar to other Torrens systems, exceptions to indefeasibility exist and may render registered

61. Taiwan Civil Code, Art. 758.
62. Taiwan Civil Code, Art. 759-1(2).

real properties defeasible. In other words, the right holder recorded in the registry is presumed to be the legitimate right holder but such presumption may be refuted by proving the exceptions such as fraud.[63] Yet the Taiwan Civil Code does not stipulate these exceptions to indefeasibility. Instead, it leaves them for judges to decide on a case-by-case basis.

77. As a matter of fact, different Torrens systems have different approaches to the exceptions to indefeasibility. As mentioned, the Taiwan Civil Code empowers the courts to determine whether any one scenario would be considered an exception and confines such exceptions to the immediate case. In comparison, Singapore's Torrens system under the Land Titles Act has largely codified such exceptions so as to limit uncertainty.[64] At the end of the day, various approaches reflect the choice of policy that inevitably involves the trade-off between the protection of the original right holder and the protection of the successor. Torrens systems with limited exceptions are inclined to protect the third party by strengthening indefeasibility of title in spite of existing defects, whereas Torrens systems that allow more exceptions are inclined to offer more protection for the original owner by operating in the opposite way.

§2. Building and Planting Rights

I. Superficies

A. General Superficies

78. In the Taiwan Civil Code, buildings, construction, and other chattels are not considered part of land. This separate ownership regime is different from that of the German Civil Code which greatly influenced Taiwan's civil-law system as a whole. As such, the owners of buildings and the owners of underlying land could be different. Owners of different units in the same condominium usually co-own the land parcels where their condominiums stand. Where the owners of condominiums are different from the owners of the underlying land, both need to have an agreement with respect to the use of the underlying land. Under the Taiwan Civil Code, *superficies* serves this purpose.

79. *Superficies* is the right to use the land of another with the purpose of constructing a building or other works.[65] *Superficies* is a proprietary right and, therefore, runs with land and can be enforced against any third party once it is registered. In practice, however, many disputes arise when building owners and landowners rely on contractual agreements (i.e., lease or lending agreement[66]) because leaseholds are not considered a proprietary interest in Taiwan. Although the Taiwan Civil

63. Taiwan Civil Code, Art. 759-1(1).
64. Land Titles Act, Singapore, Art. 46(2).
65. Taiwan Civil Code, Art. 832.
66. Taiwan Civil Code, Arts. 421, 464.

Code allows leaseholds to bind third parties when real property is succeeded under certain circumstances, leaseholds remain a contractual right and, therefore, are less effective than *superficies* in terms of binding third parties.[67]

B. Divided Superficies

80. The 2010 amendment to the Taiwan Civil Code has created a sub-category of *superficies*—divided *superficies*—to meet the need of modern city life. Divided *superficies* allow parties to create *superficies* for a certain scope of space that is vertically associated with the land of another (i.e., a designated space above or under the land parcel in question).[68] In comparison, the general *superficies* discussed earlier, which also covers the space above and beneath the land parcel, are created for buildings and other construction works on the land parcel.

C. Creation and Transfer of Superficies

81. As *superficies* is a proprietary interest, the *superficiary* (i.e., the person who owns the *superficies*) is entitled to transfer the right or create a mortgage against the *superficies* unless otherwise provided in the transfer agreement. However, to prevent over-fragmentation of property rights, such transfers of *superficies* or creation of any additional burden (e.g., mortgage) on the *superficies* have to include the buildings or any works that benefit from the *superficies* as well and cannot be separately transferred or changed.[69]

82. In a similar vein, when the landowner is to sell the underlying land parcel, Article 104 of the Land Act grants the *superficiary*/owner of buildings the right of refusal to purchase the land so that the ownership of land and the building on it is held by the same person. On the other hand, if the *superficies* is to expire or end, the owner of the underlying land parcel is entitled to purchase the building or construction at market price and the *superficiary*/owner of building cannot reject without fair reasons.[70] Where the *superficies* ends or expires, the *superficiary* is entitled to reasonable compensation for the remaining value of building or construction that will be under the landowner's effective control.[71]

83. The formalities for creating and transferring *superficies* are in line with the formalities for any other property rights under the Torrens system. The creation,

67. Taiwan Civil Code, Art. 425.
68. Taiwan Civil Code, Art. 841.
69. Taiwan Civil Code, Art. 838.
70. Taiwan Civil Code, Art. 839(3).
71. Taiwan Civil Code, Art. 840.

transfer, or any alteration of *superficies* shall not be effective unless it has been registered. Where multiple *superficies* rights exist on the same land parcel, the first registered *superficies* prevail and, therefore, the holder of *superficies* registered later can only utilize the property if the said use does not affect the first *superficiary*.[72]

84. Typically, *superficies* come with a fixed term, with rental agreed between the landowner and the *superficiary*. Where the *superficies* does not have a definite duration and has existed for more than twenty years, or the purpose of creating the *superficies* in question is no longer valid, the court may intervene upon request to determine the remaining term of the *superficies* or simply terminate the *superficies*.[73] Since the term of *superficies* is usually long, the agreed rental may fail to reflect the most updated market rate over time. If the landowner and *superficiary* fail to negotiate a revised rental, the court may also intervene to increase or reduce the rental provided unexpected changes in market conditions have rendered the rental obviously unfair.[74]

As Figure 1 shows, *superficies* has been used frequently.

Figure 1 Number of Registration Filing, Superficies, 2005–2020

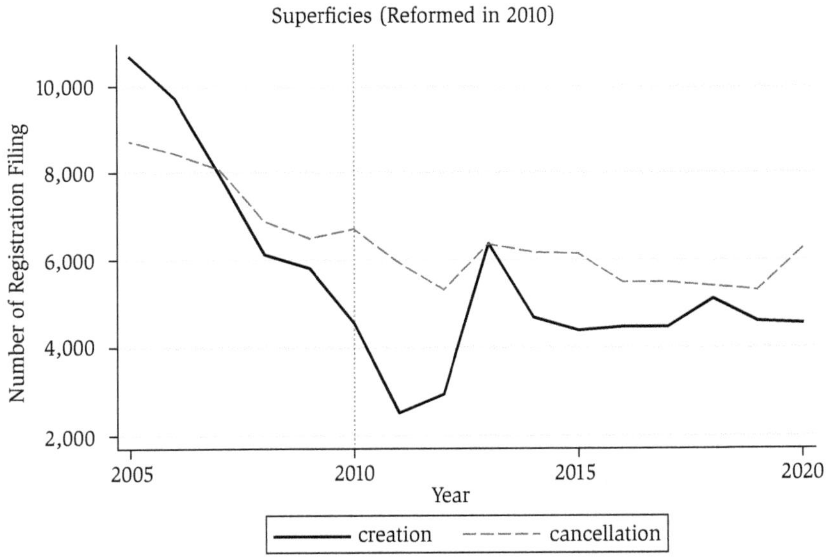

Data source: Statistical Yearbook of the Ministry of the Interior, Taiwan.
Graph created by the authors: Dotted vertical line shows the year of reform.

72. Taiwan Civil Code, Art. 841-5.
73. Taiwan Civil Code, Art. 833-1.
74. Taiwan Civil Code, Art. 835-1.

II. Agricultural Rights

A. *Concept*

85. The 2010 amendment of the Taiwan Civil Code introduced agricultural rights (alternatively, right to agricultural use) as a replacement for *emphyteusis*, or the right of permanent tenancy. The agricultural right is the right to cultivate, forest, farm, and plant on the land of another or to conserve the land.[75] As the agricultural right is a type of proprietary interest, the holder may create a mortgage against this proprietary interest.[76] That said, the holder of agricultural rights is not allowed to lease out the land or other agricultural works to a third party unless local customary laws provide otherwise.[77] The purpose of such restrictions on the alienability of agricultural rights is to simplify the legal relations underlying agricultural land use and to ensure that the right holder benefits from the agricultural rights by utilizing rather than subletting the land or agricultural works. Instead of leasing through an intermediary, any prospective land user is encouraged to acquire the agricultural right directly from the owner of land.

B. *Formality Requirement and Scope of Agricultural Rights*

86. The creation of an agricultural right and any subsequent change to such a right will not take effect without first registering the right. To ensure efficient and updated use of the land, the maximum duration of agricultural rights is limited to twenty years unless the rights are created for conservation purposes or where any law/ordinance provides otherwise.

87. Notably, the scope of agricultural rights is broader than the common-law property concept of profit à prendre, which is also associated with agricultural land use. Traditionally, profit à prendre is limited to the right to take natural resources such as minerals or timber from the land of another, whereas agricultural rights in Taiwan allow the right holder to conduct farming and ranching activities for either commercial or conservation purposes.

As Figure 2 shows, the agricultural right has not been very popular. Its users have never been many and have decreased sharply in recent years.

75. Taiwan Civil Code, Art. 850-1.
76. Taiwan Civil Code, Art. 850-3.
77. Taiwan Civil Code, Art. 850-5.

Figure 2 Number of Registration Filing, the Right of Agriculture, 2005–2020

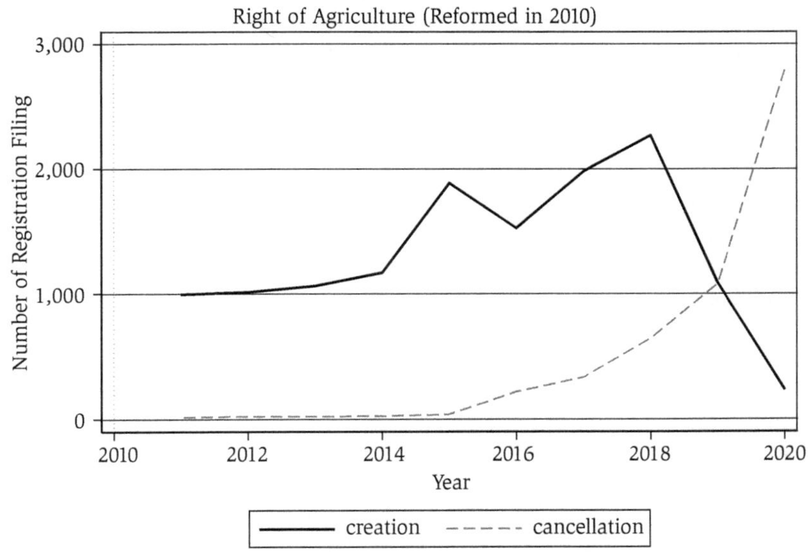

Data source: Statistical Yearbook of the Ministry of the Interior, Taiwan.
Graph created by the authors: Dotted vertical line shows the year of reform.

§3. Leasehold Interests: Chattels Real

I. The Nature of Lease

88. Under the Taiwan Civil Code, a lease is defined as a contract whereby the lessor allows the lessee to use his property in return for the rental to be paid by the lessee.[78] Notably, the object of a lease can either be immovable or movable property. Also, the interest created under a lease is merely considered a contractual rather than a proprietary interest. This is different from some common-law jurisdictions where leaseholds are considered a proprietary interest. Nevertheless, in common-law regimes, the relationship between contract and property remains debatable in the context of leases and other property law matters.[79] Occasionally, the law of leases borrows contractual principles in order to offer tenants additional protection and/or provide additional remedies. The interaction between these two areas of law generally reflects the evolution of property rights, of which many are being incrementally derived from contractual rights as illustrated by the portmanteau "chattels real."

---

78. Taiwan Civil Code, Art. 421.
79. Other such matters include, for example, proprietary estoppel or personal equity. For further discussions, *see* Kevin Gray & Susan Francis Gray, *Elements of Land Law* (Oxford Univ. Press 5th ed. 2009); Thomas W. Merrill & Henry E. Smith, *The Property/Contract Interface*, 101 Columbia L. R. 773 (2001); Thomas J. Miceli, C.F. Sirmans & Geoffrey K. Turnbull, *The Property-Contract Boundary: An Economic Analysis of Leases*, 3 Am. L. & Econ. R. 165 (2001).

89. Against this backdrop, the Taiwan Civil Code has partially "propertized" the lease interest by allowing the tenant in possession to enforce the lease against any third-party successor of the property.[80] In other words, the lease in question, similar to a property interest, binds the third-party purchaser of the leased property under certain circumstances. For example, if the lessor transfers the ownership to a third party after the lessee has obtained possession, the lease will continue to bind to the transferee.[81] In the same vein, where the landlord subsequently creates any proprietary interest (e.g., mortgage) on the leased property, it will bind the lessee if such proprietary interests hinder the lessee's right to use such property.[82] Moreover, if the lessee of land erects a building thereon and subsequently transfers the ownership of the building to a third party, the third party will be deemed as the successor of the lease and can continue to use the land under the lease.[83]

90. When a lease is created, formalities must also be adhered to for the lease to have legal effect. For example, any lease longer than one year is required to be made in writing, otherwise, it will be deemed as a periodic lease, which requires either party to give notice when he or she wants to terminate the lease.[84] In addition, to prevent the over-fragmentation of property rights, the Taiwan Civil Code grants the first right of refusal to both the lessor and lessee whenever either party would like to transfer their respective ownership so that the lessee may purchase the leased land or the lessor may purchase the building on the leased land.[85]

II. Duration

91. The Taiwan Civil Code provides that the maximum duration of a lease is twenty years. Any lease longer than twenty years is deemed as a twenty-year lease unless the lease is for the purpose of constructing buildings.[86] The Taiwan Civil Code tries to strike a balance between the utilizing property efficiently and upholding the contractual agreement made by parties.

92. In comparison, the common law generally does not impose any restriction on the length of leaseholds as long as the date of its expiry is ascertainable. Parties must ascertain when leases expire because a "fixed term" is a necessary condition

80. Taiwan Civil Code, Art. 425. For a discussion on "propertized" contractual relationship, *see* Yun-chien Chang & Henry E. Smith, *An Economic Analysis of Civil versus Common Law Property*, 88 Notre Dame L. R. 1 (2012). Similarly, for "contractualization" of the lease in the common-law context, *see* Kevin Gray & Susan Francis Gray, *Elements of Land Law* 312–313 (Oxford Univ. Press 5th ed. 2009).
81. Taiwan Civil Code, Art. 425.
82. Taiwan Civil Code, Art. 426.
83. Taiwan Civil Code, Art. 426-1.
84. Taiwan Civil Code, Arts. 422, 450.
85. Taiwan Civil Code, Art. 426-2.
86. Taiwan Civil Code, Art. 449.

for common-law leases because the fixed term distinguishes leasehold from freehold. In theory, parties may create leaseholds for as long as, for example, 9,999 years.

93. Nonetheless, the Taiwan Civil Code allows both parties to renew a lease when it expires. If the lessee continues to use the leased property after the lease expires in the absence of the lessor's objection, the lease is deemed to be renewed as a periodic lease, and the same requirement to give notice applies whenever either party wants to terminate the lease.[87]

III. Sublease

94. In principle, the lessee is not allowed to sublet the property without the lessor's consent. However, if the leased property is residential property, the tenant is allowed to sublet part of it unless any explicit covenant to not sublet the lease exists.[88] Where the lessee fails to obtain the landlord's consent or breaches any covenant not to sublet, the sublease remains effective but the lessor is entitled to terminate the head lease. In any case, the head lessee remains liable for any damage caused by the sub-lessee.

95. Generally speaking, the rules regulating subleases under the Taiwan Civil Code are similar to that under the common law, where subleases are generally permitted. Even if a covenant not to sublease explicitly exists and therefore has been breached as a result of the sublease, this does not render the sublease void unless the landlord terminates the head lease on the grounds of the breach of covenant.[89]

IV. Termination

96. A fixed-term lease ends when the lease expires, whereas a periodic lease ends when either party serves a notice to quit. Either party, however, can forfeit the lease should there be a significant breach of any covenant. For example, if a tenant fails to pay the rent, the landlord may serve a notice with a grace period and is entitled to forfeit the lease if the tenant fails to pay the rent in arrears within the designated period.[90]

97. Given the drastic nature of forfeiture, the Taiwan Civil Code requires the lessor to follow a statutorily provided procedure before forfeiture may be invoked so as to protect the lessee. The rent in arrears, for example, must be for at least two months if the leased property is a building/house, and two years for land rented for

87. Taiwan Civil Code, Art. 451.
88. Taiwan Civil Code, Art. 443.
89. *See, e.g.*, Old Grovebury Manor Farm Ltd v. W Seymour Plant Sales and Hire Ltd (No 2) [1979] 1 WLR 1397.
90. Taiwan Civil Code, Art. 440 (1).

the purpose of constructing a building/house.[91] Similar restrictions on the exercise of forfeiture by the landlord also commonly exist in common-law jurisdictions.

§4. Emphyteusis and Rent Charge

98. Emphyteusis, or the right to permanent tenancy, is a type of property right that can be traced back to imperial China. *Emphyteusis* existed in the Taiwan Civil Code until 2010 when it was replaced with the agriculture right. *Emphyteusis* divorced the right to own land and the right to use land permanently and, therefore, made the structure of property ownership very similar to that of common-law jurisdictions, in that ownership and estate are separate due to the legacy of the feudal system of Europe. *Emphyteusis* was rarely used in Taiwan particularly after the successful land reforms in the 1950s, which converged ownership and permanent tenancy, which were once commonly seen under Chinese customary law. Eventually, *emphyteusis* was abolished in 2010.

Figure 3 shows that *emphyteusis* was not popular before its abolishment.

Figure 3 Number of Registration Filing, Emphyteusis, *2005–2020*

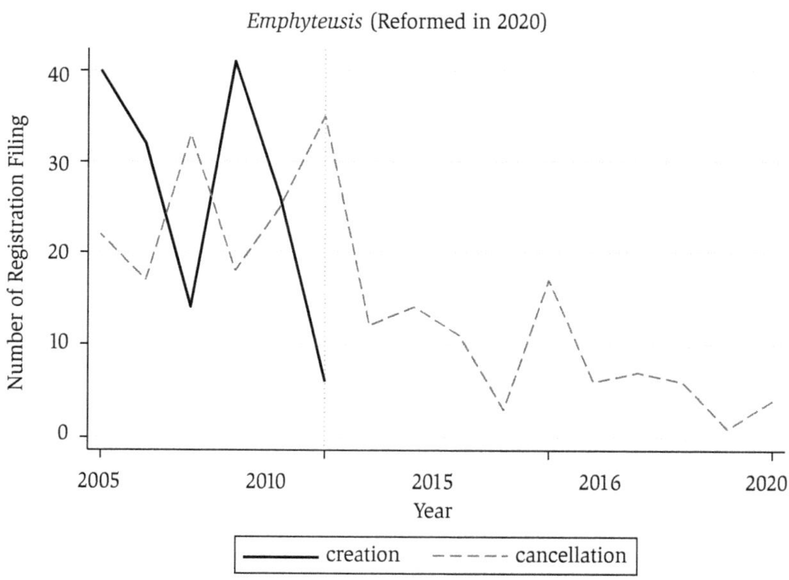

Data source: Statistical Yearbook of the Ministry of the Interior, Taiwan.
Graph created by the authors: Dotted vertical line shows the year of reform.

99. Additionally, "rent charges" are not distinct proprietary interests or rights under the Taiwan Civil Code; they are rights ancillary to claims over rent payable pursuant to leases or other contractual or proprietary arrangements. In comparison,

91. Taiwan Civil Code, Art. 440 (2).

under the common law (e.g., the UK), the rent charge is a right to revenue and creates a periodic payment which provides a continuing source of income for landowners who have permitted others to use their land for development. It is also considered a right in rem and, therefore, binds any subsequent owner of the property. The Taiwan Civil Code, however, does not recognize such a stand-alone rent charge.

§5. Use and Habitation

100. The rights of use and of habitation do not exist as individual rights under the Taiwan Civil Code. This is different from the French civil code where the rights of use and of habitation exist, and both rights provide the right holder the right to lodge in the real property of another.

101. In Taiwan, any arrangement concerning the use and habitation of real property is managed through other contractual or proprietary rights available under the Taiwan Civil Code. Generally speaking, there are three dimensions of property law that are most relevant to the use and habitation of real property in modern society: co-ownership, possession, and the landlord-tenant relationship.[92] The real property, for example, could be co-owned by husbands and wives while other family members living together enjoy the benefits of possession. They may also lease out their real property to a third party and therefore create a landlord-tenant relationship. This is particularly the case in Taiwan where many people live in apartment buildings that they purchase or rent. It is also not uncommon for married couples to live with parents or siblings.

102. Similar to the rules of "possession" in other jurisdictions, the Taiwan Civil Code protects "possession" by presuming that the possessor legally has the right in rem over the property.[93] It should be noted, however, that the possessor is defined as a person who has an effective control over the property, and this definition excludes family members, employees or any third party who merely follow the instructions of the possessor to manage or occupy the property.[94] For further discussions about co-ownership, possession, and the landlord-tenant relationship, please *see* Part I Chapter 6 and Part III Chapter 3.

92. *See* Robert Ellickson, *The Household: Informal Order Around the Hearth* 10–13 (Princeton Univ. Press 2008).
93. Taiwan Civil Code, Art. 943.
94. Taiwan Civil Code, Art. 942.

§6. Easements and Profits

I. Concept, Provision, and General Features

103. An easement is the right to use the property of another for accessing one's own property or for the purpose of drawing water, receiving light, surveying, receiving telecommunications, or for some other specific convenience while on one's own property.[95] The land which receives such a benefit is the "dominant tenement" whereas the land which provides such benefits is the "servient tenement."

104. One focus of the 2010 amendment to the Taiwan Civil Code is on easements, which commentators have long criticized for being outdated. Notably, the scope of easements has been expanded. For example, the dominant tenement and servient tenement had to be adjacent land parcels under the old regime. In comparison, under the revised definition of easement, an easement can be created between not only land parcels but also any real property such as buildings. Nonetheless, the Taiwan Civil Code only recognizes easement appurtenant but not the easement in gross that exists in some common-law jurisdictions.

105. The easements that are recognized in Taiwan are largely exhaustive under the Taiwan Civil Code. Similar efforts to codify easements can be seen in Singapore under the Land Titles Act, which codified various easements created by case law. Given the diverse methods of land use, the objects of easement are equally diverse, including easements for parking, lodging, right of way, light, storage, access, etc. As the easement is a property interest and can be enforced against third parties, courts should and are often slow to recognize any new type of easement. Disputes often arise when parties argue for a new easement based on customs, market practices, or implicit agreements concerning land use. As such, the purpose of codification is to provide clear guidance about the types of easements available and to formally introduce easements recognized by customary law and/or case law into the Torrens system.

II. Creation of Easements

106. For an easement to be created between two parties, it needs to be made in writing, and the easement takes effect only after registration. Additionally, easements can be created by acquisitive prescription. Any person who has peacefully, publicly, and continually possessed another person's property for ten years with the intent of being an owner, and who acts in good faith without any negligence since commencing possession, is entitled to be registered as the holder of the easement over the servient tenement. In Taiwan, it should be noted that the easement by

95. Taiwan Civil Code, Art. 851.

acquisitive prescription trumps the indefeasibility of title provided by the Torrens system and such easement also applies to registered land.[96]

107. The existence of an easement does not prevent the owner of servient tenement from creating other proprietary interests in his land as long as the existing easement is not affected. It should also be noted that any easement and its servient tenement cannot be separately transferred.[97] This restriction on the transferability of easements reflects the policy consideration of simplifying property ownership.

108. Figure 4 shows that, somewhat surprisingly, even real easement has been used very infrequently.

Figure 4 Number of Registration Filing, Real Easement, 2005–2020

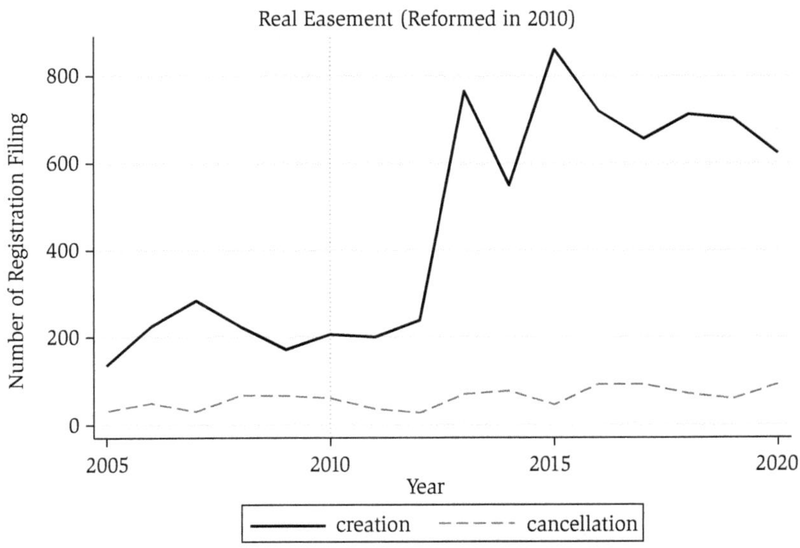

Data source: Statistical Yearbook of the Ministry of the Interior, Taiwan.
Graph created by the authors: Dotted vertical line shows the year of reform.

96. Taiwan Civil Code, Art. 772. In comparison, Singapore's Torrens system does not recognize the applicability of prescriptive acquisition of any proprietary interest for registered land. Registration serves as conclusive evidence of ownership and other proprietary interests. Land Titles Act of Singapore, Art. 36. For a further discussion in Taiwan's context, *see* Yun-chien Chang, *Venerable or Outdated? A Radical Proposal to Reform Prescriptive Acquisition Law in Taiwan*, 18 Academia Sinica L. J. 195 (2016).
97. Tsay-chuan Hsieh, *Civil Code Property II* 135–136 (New Sharing Publishing 2010); Kuang-ming Wu, *New Civil Code Property* 385 (San Min Publishing 2009).

III. Statutory Easements and Natural Rights

109. The Taiwan Civil Code has also codified a number of implied easements that have been widely recognized by case law in common-law jurisdictions. Easement by necessity, for example, is a statutory easement that grants the owner of landlocked property access to a public road through the adjacent property of third parties.[98] In practice, however, such easements are not common in Taiwan.[99]

110. Additionally, the Taiwan Civil Code codifies a number of natural rights that are often discussed together with easements in common-law jurisdictions. For example, the right to use any water naturally found on land is provided by Article 775 of the Taiwan Civil Code. Article 774 also provides for the right to support, which gives landowners the right to have their properties supported by land adjacent to theirs. Nonetheless, the Taiwan Civil Code organizes these natural rights in a slightly different way from its common-law counterparts. In Taiwan, such natural rights are incorporated into the Taiwan Civil Code as part of a bundle of obligations generally imposed on landowners rather than a set of individual property rights.[100]

IV. Profits

111. The common-law concept of "profits" (or *profits à prendre*) is similar to the concept of "easement"—both are proprietary interests in land and related to the right to use the land of another. Nonetheless, profits differ from easements in that profits do not require a dominant tenement. Also, profits refer to the right to enter land and profiteer from such land. For example, the right holder of profits may own no land but is entitled to the benefits thereon, such as profits to fish or fell wood. In comparison, the easement traditionally requires the existence of both dominant and servient tenements and gives an easement holder the right to use the servient tenement for a variety of purposes, which are not limited to profiteering out of the land.

112. After the 2010 amendment to the Taiwan Civil Code, which expanded the applicability of easements, the right to profiteer is, in principle, recognized under the Taiwan Civil Code as a form of easement. An easement currently can be also created for the benefit of not only real property owners but also holders of leasehold or other proprietary interests in the servient tenement who want to benefit from the servient tenement.[101] In this way, the definition of easement under the Taiwan Civil Code is so wide that some easements may now be created without a dominant tenement, much like the concept of profits. That said, this type of easement remains

98. Taiwan Civil Code, Art. 787. *See* Yun-chien Chang, *Hybrid Rule: Hidden Entitlement Protection Rule in Access to Landlocked Land Doctrine*, 88 TUL. L. REV. 217 (2016).
99. Yun-chien Chang, *An Empirical Study of Legal Servitude of Passage Cases in Taiwan*, 216 Taiwan L. R. 211 (2013).
100. For example, Art. 774 states that "in carrying on business and in exercising one's ownership, the landowner shall take necessary care to prevent any damage to the adjacent land." Taiwan Civil Code, Art. 774.
101. Taiwan Civil Code, Art. 859-3.

different from profits because the said easement holder has to own certain proprietary interests in the servient tenement before he or she can create such an easement.

§7. LICENSES

113. Licenses under the Taiwan Civil Code, like those in common-law jurisdictions, are viewed as contractual interests. The Taiwan Civil Code provides several general provisions with respect to bare licenses. These bare licenses justify certain types of occupations that may otherwise be viewed as trespass. For example, Article 790 stipulates two exceptions to trespass: (1) when other persons are entitled to pass through the land; and (2) when local customs allow other persons to enter the owner's unfenced land for the purpose of felling wood, harvesting crops, gathering abandoned timber, foraging for food, or allowing stock to graze. Also, the landowner shall allow the person who owns or possesses inanimate objects or animals, which have by accident entered the land, to enter the land to retrieve them.[102]

114. Notably, the issues concerning licenses are often about the proprietary nature of licenses as the case may be. The question is, under what circumstances do licenses (particularly, contractual license or licenses arising by estoppel) amount to a proprietary interest so that the licensee can claim damages from the licensor and/ or enforce license interests against a third party? These issues concern another function of license theory; that is, to grant the licensee an action for damages if a license is subsequently revoked, since the licensee may have made improvements to the property. Damages may also arise as a result of the licensee's reliance on the revoked license.

115. These issues usually arise from the underlying relation that gives rise to the license interests in question. In a sense, the label "licenses" is misleading because "license" is merely incidental and ancillary to the right that has actually been granted over the land. For this reason, different property regimes apply varying approaches. Common-law jurisdictions have applied, for example, the doctrine of proprietary estoppel to deal with them within the realm of property law. In Taiwan, the Civil Code leaves these issues to the areas of law concerning the underlying legal relationship that create license interests, such as contract, torts, and restitution.

116. With respect to the damages given when licenses are revoked, the Taiwan Civil Code applies law of contract (which includes torts and restitution) as a remedy instead of developing any further rules for licenses. Given the nature of licenses in Taiwan, the licensee does not have an action for specific performance nor a right to prevent the transfer of the property to a third party. However, if the licensee would like to claim compensation for the improvements made to the property, he or

102. Taiwan Civil Code, Art. 791.

she can rely on Article 179 of the Taiwan Civil Code on a ground of unjust enrichment. Article 179 provides that a person who acquires an interest in property without any legal basis, or if any existing legal basis is subsequently revoked, the recipient (e.g., the licensor who revokes the license) shall pay compensation to the creator of such interests.

117. Article 179 provides the definition of unjust enrichment as follows: "A person who is benefited, without any legal ground, at the expense of others, is obliged to return the benefit. The same rule shall apply, if a legal ground existed but ceased to exist subsequently." Unjust enrichment is distinguishable from tort liability in that it requires no unlawful act or fault on the part of the benefited party. The benefited party's obligation arises only where he is enriched, whereas the tortfeasor's liability arises from the harm he has caused, irrespective of whether he has benefited from the injured party's loss. More specifically, unjust enrichment occurs where the following elements are present: (1) One party (the "benefited party") is enriched by acquiring benefits; (2) The enrichment occurs at the expense of another party (the "injured party"); (3) There are no legal grounds for the benefited party's enrichment.

118. As for (1), a person may become enriched by possessing, owning, or holding in his name another person's corporeal things, money, company shares, etc. For instance, if Peter intended to transfer money to Paul's bank account, but instead put the money in Mary's bank account, Mary is enriched. The relevant issue is simply the fact of enrichment: no element as to the state of mind of either party has to be demonstrated on the question of whether there has been an enrichment. A person may become enriched even if the disposition by which they receive property is void (for example, under Article 118). In other words, a party in possession of property may be enriched, even though that party did not acquire ownership. The effect in that scenario is that Taiwanese law continues to regard the property in the possession of the recipient as being owned by the person to whom it belonged prior to the void transaction; so that the latter may bring a claim of unjust enrichment against the former.

119. As for (2), enrichment that does not come at the expense of the injured party cannot give rise to a claim to return or compensate the injured party's loss.

120. As for (3), a legal ground for enrichment may, for instance, be the existence of a valid contract or operation of a legal rule.

121. Moreover, where any further damage is caused to the licensee, the licensee is entitled to claim damages in tort pursuant to Article 184 of the Taiwan Civil Code. Article 184, the general provision dealing with torts, provides that any person who, intentionally or negligently, causes damage to the rights of another shall pay compensation for any damage and injury therefrom. Furthermore, any person who intentionally causes any damage and injury to another person in a manner against the rule of morals or equity shall be liable for such damage even if the victim does not possess a legal right that is recognized under the Taiwan Civil Code. As such, the licensee can sue for damages against the licensor or a third party that is liable under Article 184 even if the licensee has only a personal right rather than a proprietary right.

§8. Restrictive Covenants

122. Easements and restrictive covenants may overlap functionally when they are created to restrict the use of the land of another. Nonetheless, several differences between restrictive covenants and easements remain prominent. Easements are property interests whereas restrictive covenants are considered contractual interests. Easements bind third parties but restrictive covenants do not except in certain circumstances where a third party has been served with notice. Restrictive covenants are often created by express instead of implied agreements and would be stipulated in writing in agreements. In contrast, easements would be established explicitly or implicitly, and many disputes concern implied easements as they are not formalized in writing. Additionally, one cannot acquire a restrictive covenant by prescription, necessity, or estoppel.

123. As in other jurisdictions, however, the distinction between the two concepts is not always clear to ordinary property owners and disputes may arise because the parties fail to arrange their proprietary interests in a way that is acceptable to them.

124. In Taiwan, the Condominium Administration Act and the 2010 amendment to the Taiwan Civil Code allow developers and residents to create covenants for the purpose of planning and managing condominiums. Notably, such covenants run with real properties and bind successors with notice of such covenants (*see, e.g.*, Article 826-1). Here, the required notice is not limited to the actual notice but also includes constructive notice. Pursuant to the Condominium Administration Act, before properties in question are purchased, any potential buyer/transferee is entitled to review the existing covenants. Therefore, all successors would have actual notice of restrictive covenants, if any, or would be deemed to have constructive notice as they have been given the opportunity to review.[103]

125. Moreover, Article 859-4 of the Taiwan Civil Code allows the real property owner to create an easement over his own property. In this way, the owner's decision on how his real property (e.g., for conservation purposes) should be utilized will bind his successors. Such self-created easements go beyond the scope of traditional easements, which require both dominant and servient tenements, and this functionally overlaps with restrictive covenants that run with real property.

---

103. For relevant issues in the context of condominium living, *see* Yun-chien Chang, *Condominium Law in Taiwan: Doctrinal Overview under the Lens of Information-Cost Theory*, 23 Asia Pacific L. Rev. 89, 107 (2015).

§9. DIAN

I. Concept and Provisions

126. *Dian* is a property right derived from the Chinese agricultural economy dating back to imperial China. *Dian* is the right to use and collect profits on the real property of another for a term not longer than thirty years.[104] The *dian*-holder can utilize real property and have exclusive possession of it as if he or she were the owner, whereas the *dian*-maker retains ownership of the property and has the right to redeem the property at the price the *dian* was originally created.[105]

127. During the term of *dian*, the *dian*-holder can create a sub-*dian* for a third party so long as the term of the sub-*dian* is no longer than the original *dian*.[106] That said, the Taiwan Civil Code prohibits excessive divergence of property rights from being created. For example, *dian* as a property right is transferable, and the *dian* itself can be the object of a mortgage. However, where the land under *dian* and the building thereon are owned by different persons (e.g., the *dian*-holder may construct residential property on land under *dian* and take ownership of such property), the building and the *dian* right both have to be transferred to the same successor together if any transfer were to take place.[107] On the other hand, the *dian*-maker can subsequently create other proprietary rights against his ownership, such as a mortgage, so long as such right will not affect the exercise of any right by the *dian*-holder.[108] For example, the owner can set a mortgage against the land under *dian*, which he does not possess anymore. But if the owner defaults on his mortgage payment and, consequently, the land is transferred to a third party as a result of the mortgagee's right to sell a mortgaged property, the third party's right to ownership is subject to the existing *dian*.[109]

II. Social Meaning of Dian

128. *Dian* is a type of property right that was not transplanted from Germany, Switzerland, or Japan but derived locally. Before the 2010 amendment to the Taiwan Civil Code, some commentators suggested that *dian* should be abolished on the ground that *superficies* and leases could sufficiently play the role that *dian* once played in the agricultural economy of imperial China. Nonetheless, the Taiwan Civil Code kept the concept of *dian* but clarified its scope and reconciled it with other modern property rights.

129. *Dian* reflects a fundamental aspect of Chinese agricultural society in that *dian* helps liquidize the property interests in land that was once monopolized by

104. Taiwan Civil Code, Arts. 911, 912.
105. Taiwan Civil Code, Art. 923.
106. Taiwan Civil Code, Art. 915.
107. Taiwan Civil Code, Art. 917(2).
108. Judicial Yuan Interpretation No. 139.
109. Taiwan Civil Code, Art. 917.

family clans and viewed as part of a family's legacy rather than a transferable commodity. In this regard, the nature and features of a society are revealed through the history and nature of property rights.[110] In imperial China, owners of family land might have needed to capitalize their land but were not willing to do so by an outright sale. Consequently, *dian* served as an alternative vehicle to get the capital that these owners needed while keeping nominal ownership for the sake of maintaining their family's reputation. Against this backdrop, *dian* is at odds with property theory derived from the Western capitalist economy. Some commentators hold a view that the complexity of *dian* and its non-market-oriented redemption right may have hindered the development of the Chinese agricultural economy.[111] For example, to redeem and recover the land, the *dian*-maker could simply pay the same price that the *dian*-holder paid, say, thirty years ago. Such design fails to reflect market conditions, such as inflation, and imposes great uncertainty on the *dian*-holder.[112] However, these concerns may not be necessary in the context of Chinese agricultural economy where *dian* was created as a substitute for sale and, therefore, redemption rights were more symbolic.[113]

130. Viewing *dian* from a social and historical perspective helps explain certain configurations of the rights created by *dian*. In a close-knit agricultural society, parties involved in *dian* and members of the local community are usually clear as to who will own the property if the *dian*-maker fails to redeem the property under *dian* before the *dian* expires. Where *dian* is longer than fifteen years, both parties may choose to covenant that non-redeemed property will be deemed as sold on the date of expiration and that the person who receives the *dian* will be entitled to be registered as the owner.[114] Also, when the *dian*-maker fails to redeem the *dian* two years after the fixed-term *dian* expires, or thirty years after the *dian* without fixed term was created, the *dian*-holder will be deemed as the owner of such property.[115] As such, the Taiwan Civil Code injects much certainty into this area of the law by formalizing both parties' intentions to pursue a complete transfer of the property interests.

131. Similarly, where the real property under *dian* is wholly or partially destroyed by an act amounting to force majeure during the duration of *dian*, the Taiwan Civil Code allocates the risk of loss to both parties in a simple and clear manner based on the status quo: the *dian*-holder bears the loss of his right to use the real

---

110. H. F. Schurmann, *Traditional Property Concepts in China*, 15 J. Asian Stud. 507 (1956).
111. Robert Ellickson, *The Costs of Complex Land Titles: Two Examples from China*, 1 Property Rights Conf. J. 281 (2012).
112. *Ibid.*
113. For comparison of Chinese *dian* and English mortgage, *see* Taisu Zhang, *The Laws and Economics of Confucianism* (Cambridge Univ. Press 2017).
114. Taiwan Civil Code, Art. 913.
115. Taiwan Civil Code, Arts. 923, 924.

property and cannot request the return of consideration pro-rata, whereas the *dian*-maker bears the loss of his real property.[116] In other words, both the right of redemption and *dian* are extinguished with respect to the part of the real property destroyed. This is similar to the allocation of risk between the seller and buyer after the sale and transfer has been completed.

Figure 5 shows that *dian* is pretty much dead. Unreported table would show that most of the *dian* users are in Kinmen, an offshore island that has never been colonized by Japan. By contrast, the practice of using *dian* in the Taiwan Island was destroyed when, during the Japanese colonial period, *dian* was converted to *antichresis*.

Figure 5 Number of Registration Filing, Dian, *2005–2020*

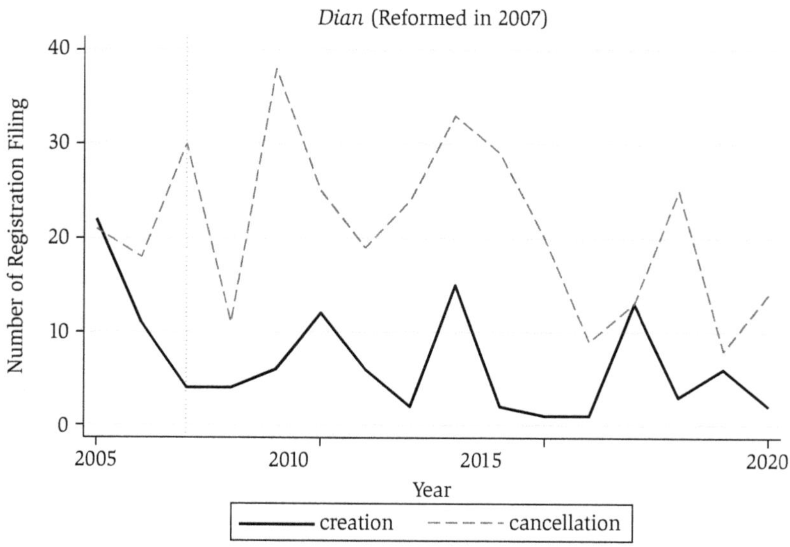

Data source: Statistical Yearbook of the Ministry of the Interior, Taiwan.
Graph created by the authors: Dotted vertical line shows the year of reform.

116. Taiwan Civil Code, Arts. 920, 921.

Chapter 5. Security Interests

132. In this monograph, we use "security rights" rather than "security (interests)" or "securities" to refer to mortgage, pledge, and lien. "Security rights" are a better translation of the Chinese term used in the Taiwan Civil Code. Security rights in real property include ordinary mortgage and line-of-credit mortgage, transplanted from the Japanese Civil Code. For a detailed introduction of mortgages, *see* Part VI. For a brief introduction of mortgages, *see* Chapter 3 of Part I.

Chapter 6. Concurrent Ownership

§1. Concurrent Ownership of Immovable Property

I. In General

A. *Classification: Tenancy in Common and Joint and Indivisible Ownership*

133. There are three types of co-ownership (coterminous with concurrent ownership) forms under Taiwan law: tenancy in common, joint and indivisible ownership, and condominium. Condominium is explained in §2, whereas the first two are introduced in §1 and §3. A joint and indivisible ownership can only be created according to statutory stipulation or custom.[117] For instance, partnership property,[118] certain marital property,[119] and inherited property before partition[120] are held in joint and indivisible ownership. All other things can in principle be held in tenancy in common.

1. Shares: Definition and Transfer

134. Tenants in common own things according to their shares.[121] Shares, if unclear, would be presumed equal among co-tenants.[122] Each co-tenant can unilaterally transfer his or her share.[123] Co-tenants share the benefits, profits, or burdens pro-rata.[124] By contrast, the concept of shares is not applicable to joint and indivisible ownership. Co-owners in joint and indivisible ownership own things together and as a whole.[125] That is, they cannot transfer their "shares" (i.e., co-owner status) at will.

2. Co-owned Properties: Administration

135. Administration of things held in tenancy in common is in principle determined by a majority vote.[126] More exactly, if more than 50% of the co-owners own more than 50% of the shares, they can administer the things according to their own

117. Taiwan Civil Code, Art. 827.
118. Taiwan Civil Code, Art. 667.
119. Taiwan Civil Code, Art. 1031.
120. Taiwan Civil Code, Art. 1151.
121. Taiwan Civil Code, Art. 817.
122. Taiwan Civil Code, Art. 817.
123. Taiwan Civil Code, Art. 819.
124. Taiwan Civil Code, Arts. 818, 822.
125. Taiwan Civil Code, Art. 827.
126. Taiwan Civil Code, Art. 820.

plans.[127] Co-tenants, by consensus, can adopt other quorum rules. Co-owners dissenting with the "obviously unfair" management plan can petition the court to alter it.[128]

136. Simple repairs and other similar preservation acts can be done by any co-owner unilaterally.[129] Similarly, any co-tenant can unilaterally reclaim from, or bring a revindication lawsuit against, a third party as long as it is for the benefit of all co-owners as a whole.[130]

137. Administration of things held in joint and indivisible ownership is stipulated in Article 828 of the Taiwan Civil Code, paragraph 1 of which stipulates that the rights and duties of co-owners are determined by the relevant rules (such as those of partnership) which apply to that relationship. In the case of joint and indivisible ownership due to inheritance, neither Book 5 of the Taiwan Civil Code nor other relevant statutes contain more specific stipulations in respect of the heirs' joint and indivisible ownership. In the absence of such provisions, paragraph 2 of Article 828 should apply.

138. Paragraph 2 of Article 828 stipulates that Articles 820, 821, and 826-1 (introduced in paragraphs 136 and 137) should apply *mutatis mutandis* to joint tenancies.

139. If paragraph 2 of Article 828 were considered inapplicable, paragraph 3 of Article 828 would apply. This provides that, unless otherwise stipulated, consensus among co-owners is required.

140. The stipulations regarding co-ownership in the Taiwan Civil Code (introduced above) typically apply to ownership of corporeal (i.e., tangible) things.

141. Pursuant to Article 831, these rules apply to limited property rights in corporeal things (such as mortgage, etc.). A number of scholars agree that Article 831 extends to incorporeal (i.e., intangible) things,[131] including, most importantly, company shares and "obligational right" (a concept borrowed from German law; a contractual claim, a tort damages claim, or an unjust enrichment claim are typical examples). Article 831 uses the term "quasi-co-ownership" to describe this kind of non-standard co-ownership.

---

127. Co-owners who own more than two-thirds of the shares have the same power. Taiwan Civil Code, Art. 820.
128. Taiwan Civil Code, Art. 820.
129. Taiwan Civil Code, Art. 820.
130. Taiwan Civil Code, Art. 821.
131. *See* Tsay-chuan Hsieh, *Property Law: Volume 1* 461–465 (Tsay-chuan Hsieh 7th ed. 2020); Tez-chien Wang, *Property Law* 334 (Tez-chien Wang 2d ed. 2010) [in Chinese].

142. Quasi-co-ownership of claims often arises in the inheritance context, so claims are held in joint and indivisible ownership.[132] A number of commentators agree that the key is to determine whether a co-owner exercising a claim is analogous to a property owner exercising his *rei vindicatio* claim, as stipulated in Article 821 (a *rei vindicatio* claim being a claim for the return of property). If it is, pursuant to paragraph 2 of Article 828 and Article 821, a co-owner may unilaterally bring claims for the benefits of all co-owners. If it is not, pursuant to paragraph 3 of Article 828, all co-owners have to consent.

143. The jurisprudence of the Taiwan Supreme Court was split prior to, and remains split after, the Third Civil Division Meeting Resolution (1) of the Supreme Court (2015) (hereinafter, the "2015 Resolution").[133] The 2015 Resolution decided that paragraph 3 of Article 828 is the applicable rule, as a bare majority of the participants of the meeting considered that exercising a claim against an obligor was not a type of a claim for restoration, and thus that paragraph 2 of Article 828 and Article 821 were not applicable. Therefore, in principle (albeit with important exceptions; *see* below), the 2015 Resolution decided that consensus among co-owners is required to exercise a co-owned claim. This, however, requires some qualification and caution.

144. Before, and even *after*, the 2015 Resolution was announced, Taiwan's Supreme Court expressed a view different from the one set out in the 2015 Resolution. For instance, Supreme Court Judgment 2010 Tai-Kang-Tze No. 979, Supreme Court Judgment 2013 Tai-Shang-Tze No. 1307, Supreme Court Judgment 2015 Tai-Shang-Tze No. 554, and Supreme Court Judgment 2015 Tai-Shang-Tze No. 248 all held that one co-owner of a claim is entitled to file lawsuits alone, a position clearly different from the 2015 Resolution.[134]

145. The 2015 Resolution was made in light of a long line of court precedents that carve out exceptions to paragraph 3 of Article 828. Prof. Chung-Jau Wu has written three articles on this issue.[135] Prof. Wu points out that the Supreme Court

---

132. Taiwan Civil Code, Art. 1148 stipulates that "Unless otherwise stipulated in this Code, upon the commencement of succession, an heir assumes all the rights and duties pertaining to the patrimony of the deceased, except those rights and duties which exclusively belong to the decedent. An heir's duties to settle the obligations of the decedent are limited to the extent of the inherited estate." The word "estate" in Art. 1148 refers only to assets (of positive value), but not liabilities. Under Art. 1148, the decedent's rights and duties (put differently, their assets and liabilities) immediately pass to his heirs upon his death, albeit in their separate patrimonies. Art. 1151 of the Taiwan Civil Code stipulates that "where there are several heirs, the whole of the deceased's assets is, before its partition, joint and indivisibly owned by the heirs." Accordingly, the heirs own the assets (i.e. the estate) and liabilities as co-owners.

133. As said above, Civil Division Meeting Resolutions are no longer considered a de jure authority.

134. *See* Chung-Jau Wu, "The Exercise of Joint Claims: A Comment on the Third Civil Division Meeting Resolution (1) of Supreme Court (2015)," *Chinese and German Civil Law Research* 14 (2016): 185–186.

135. *See id*; Chung-Jau Wu, "Exercising Claims Held in Joint and Indivisible Ownership and the Missing Mandatory Joint Lawsuit", in *Focal Forum on Civil Procedural Law* 51–71; Chung-Jau Wu, "Interaction of the Article 56-1 of the Civil Procedure Act and Article 828 of the Civil Code", Taiwan Law Journal 201 (2012), 75–92.

has always (before and after the 2015 Resolution) made exceptions to the doctrine of consensus among co-owners of claims. The exception, as Prof. Wu calls it, is the "cannot realistically get all joint claimants to agree" formula. That is, if some co-owners of the claim other than the co-owner who seeks to be the plaintiff of the claim purposefully refuse to be listed as plaintiffs, explicitly oppose the plaintiff filing the lawsuit, or have conflicting interests, the would-be plaintiff cannot realistically get the other co-owners of the claim to agree to be listed as plaintiffs. *Consequently, the plaintiff who is one of the co-owners of the claim still has standing in the lawsuit.* Numerous Supreme Court cases, including many that were rendered after the 2015 Resolution, take this position. Therefore, one should understand the 2015 Resolution against the background of the jurisprudence of the Taiwan Supreme Court. The adopted view in the 2015 Resolution requires all co-owners of a claim to file a lawsuit together *only when it is realistic to do so.* The purpose of such a view is to give all co-owners of a claim proper notice of ongoing lawsuits, while not stopping one or some of the co-owners of a claim from filing lawsuits when other co-owners are against the co-owner who seeks to bring that claim *qua* plaintiff.

146. Still, scholars criticized the 2015 Resolution and the Supreme Court decisions that led to it.

147. Justice Tai-Lang Lu argues that Article 293 of the Taiwan Civil Code should apply when multiple successors hold a claim jointly.[136] According to Article 293,[137] any joint obligee can make a claim on behalf of all joint obligees, if such a claim directs the duty holder to pay to all joint obligees as a whole. Prof. Rong-Chwan Chen also holds the view that Article 293 should be the governing rule for co-owned claims, as Article 831 (which applies Article 828 when rights over property other than ownership are held as co-owners or tenants in common by co-owners) refers only to property rights, not claims.[138] Justice Lu and Prof. Chen consider the Civil Code sections on tenancy in common and joint and indivisible ownership (Articles 820–831) to be rules designed for property rights, and thus the provisions of the Book of Obligation in the Civil Code (such as Article 293) should apply to obligational claims held in joint and indivisible ownership.

---

136. *See* Tai-Lang Lu, "The Possibility of Unilateral Actions by Joint Claimants or Joint Debtors: Analysis of Several Supreme Court Judgements," *in New Thoughts on Property Law and Civil Laws: Essays in Honor of Former Vice-President of Judicial Yuan Hsieh Tsay-Chuan's 70th Birthday* 137 (the Editorial Board for Festschrift for Justice Tsay-chuan Hsieh ed., Angle 2014); Tai-Lang Lu, "The Standing of Joint Claimants in Payment Lawsuits: A Comment on the Third Civil Division Meeting Resolution (1) of Supreme Court (2015)," *Court Case Times* 49 (2016).

137. Paragraph 1 of Art. 293 stipulates that "If there are several persons entitled to a claim which is indivisible in nature, each obligee may enforce it on behalf of all obligees; and the obligor shall tender the performance to all obligees." A typical indivisible claim is, for instance, that Peter, Paul, and Mary jointly purchase a car from BMW. Peter, Paul, or Mary alone may demand that BMW deliver the said car, but the car has to be delivered to all three together. At the enforcement stage, court marshalls have to ensure that the car is entrusted to all three persons or the person(s) designated by them.

138. *See* Rong-Chwan Chen, "Exercise the Claims Held in Joint and Indivisible Ownership: Comments and Analysis on the Resolution of the Supreme Court," *Taiwan Law Journal* 400 (2020): 93.

148. Many scholars hold the view that claims from an estate are held in quasi-joint and indivisible ownership by all successors, and any one of them may exercise the claim. Justice Tsay-chuan Hsieh chaired the task force that drafted the amended articles in the Book of Things in Taiwan's Civil Code. His understanding of the addition of paragraph 2 of Article 828 in 2009 is that it was to enable co-owners of a claim to make a claim individually on behalf of all of the co-owners.[139]

149. Other scholars may adopt different reasoning, but their conclusion is the same: namely, that *any co-owner of a claim can make the claim on behalf of all co-owners.*[140] One article notably points out that tenants in common are able to unilaterally demand partition of co-owned assets (Article 823). Co-owners, by contrast, are not allowed to dissolve the joint and indivisible ownership at will. Therefore, given the straightjacket provided by the rules regarding joint and indivisible ownership, it is even more important to enable co-owners to seek redress individually, rather than disabling them.[141]

150. We would add that joint tenancies arising in the contexts of marital property, partnership, and inheritance may be treated differently. Policy makers may have wider policy considerations in requiring consensus in the context of a marriage or a partnership (such as ensuring the stability of those ongoing relationships). By contrast, joint and indivisible ownership of an estate is clearly a transitional arrangement. The goal of the succession law is, as quickly as possible, to ascertain the whereabouts of all the property in the estate, make claims, repay debts, and then finally distribute the remaining estate to the heir or heirs. Constructing hurdles in the way of making claims and prolonging the process makes little policy sense in this context.

---

139. The sixth edition of Justice Hsieh's textbook clearly points out that one joint claimant alone can make a claim on behalf of all the joint claimants. *See* Tsay-chuan Hsieh, *Property Law: Vol. 1* 392, 443 (Tsay-chuan Hsieh 6th ed. 2014). The seventh edition of Justice Hsieh's textbook continues to criticize the 2015 Resolution. *See* Tsay-chuan Hsieh, *Property Law: Vol. 1* 463 (Tsay-chuan Hsieh 7th ed. 2020).

    Para. 1 of Art. 828 takes precedence over para. 2 of Art. 828, which further takes precedence over para. 3 of Art. 828. See Wen-hui Chiu, *Commentary on the Rights in Rem under the Civil Code* 174–177 (Angle 2020).

140. *See* Chien-wei Wang, *The Exercise of Joint Claims*, 160 Taiwan Jurist 69 (2016); Chen-erh Lin, *Claiming Joint Claims: A Comment on the Supreme Court Judgment 2015 Tai-Shang-Tze No. 2184*, 45 Court Case Times 15 (2016); Chin-fa You, *Vindication System* 109, 117, 128 (Angle 2d ed. 2016); Wen-hui Chiu, *Commentary on the Rights in Rem under the Civil Code* 151–153 (Angle, 2020). Prof. Tsung-Jung Liu calls for further legislative reform to clearly give a joint claimant the right to file lawsuits alone. *See* Tsung-Jung Liu, *A Discussion on the Right of Co-heirs to the Claims in Common*, 244 Taiwan L. Rev. 73–75 (2015).

141. *See* Rong-Chwan Chen, *Exercise the Claims Held in Joint and Indivisible Ownership: Comments and Analysis on the Resolution of the Supreme Court*, 400 Taiwan L. J. 400 (2020): 86.

151. Civil procedure scholars have also discussed this legal issue extensively.[142] As analyzed by Prof. Kuo-chang Huang, courts have refused to add co-owners with conflicting interests as co-plaintiffs and have instead allowed the co-owner to proceed with the lawsuit.[143]

3. Co-owned Properties: Conveyance

152. Co-owners can sell or use co-owned things as collateral only through consensual agreements.[144] Article 34-1 of the Land Act prescribes, however, that co-owned land or co-owned buildings can be sold or burdened by *superficies* by a majority vote of co-owners. More exactly, if more than 50% of the co-owners own more than 50% of the shares, they can convey the property rights according to their own plans.[145]

B. Partition

1. Unilateral Right to Petition for Partition

153. A co-tenant in principle can demand partition at any time.[146] Co-tenants have to attempt voluntary partition before seeking judicial partition. Should such a negotiation fail, any co-owner can petition courts to partition the co-ownership unilaterally.[147] An empirical study shows that in 2005–2010, at least 82.5% of the co-ownership partitions were conducted through voluntary agreements, mediation, and settlements, while only about 7.5% of the partitions were ordered by courts.[148]

2. Partition Approaches

154. The substance of the judicial partition doctrine has changed substantially. Before January 2009, the old Taiwan Civil Code Article 824 authorized the court to partition co-owned properties in kind or by sale, without preferring either approach. The court was also allowed to adopt an intermediate approach. For instance, courts can order partition in kind and award monetary compensation (called "owelty" in

142. *See* Yu-xiu Chen et al., *The Standing in Litigations regarding Joint Claims Acquired by Inheritance: With Comments on the View Adopted in Third Civil Division Meeting Resolution (1) of Supreme Court (2015) (The Minute of the 131st Civil Procedure Law)*, 245 L. J. 143–196 (2017).
143. *See* Kuo-chang Huang, *Reexamination of the Involuntary Plaintiff Device: An Empirical Analysis*, 38 Natl Taiwan U. L. J. 102–104 38 (2009).
144. Taiwan Civil Code, Arts. 819, 828.
145. Co-owners who own more than two-thirds of the shares have the same power. *See* Land Act, Art. 34-1.
146. Taiwan Civil Code, Art. 823.
147. *Ibid.*
148. Yun-chien Chang, *Tenancy in "Anticommons"? A Theoretical and Empirical Analysis of Co-Ownership*, 4 J. Legal Analysis 515 (2012).

common law) to the co-tenants who do not receive property according to their shares. Article 824 was revised in 2009. The new law prefers partition in kind, but at the same time allows the court to order several more types of "partial partition" when physically dividing the real estate pro-rata is not feasible.

155. To give an example of partial partition, suppose persons ABC and D co-own Blackacre and ABCE co-own Whiteacre; the court may, upon ABC's request, partition Blackacre and Whiteacre together. The verdict could look like the following: ABCD continue to co-own part of Blackacre; ACE co-own half of White-acre; each of ABCD receives some part of Blackacre, but not according to their shares, so AB have to compensate CD; and the other half of Whiteacre will be auctioned and ABCE will divide the proceeds pro-rata.

156. The district courts in Taiwan have rendered approximately one thousand verdicts on co-ownership partitioning each year. Empirical studies of court verdicts reveal that during 2008–2010, in the Court of First Instance in Taiwan, partition in kind and partition by sale were used 25% and 20% of the time, respectively; in a majority of the cases, the court broke up the tenancy in common by combining all or some of the following approaches: partition in kind, partition by sale, owelty, and continued co-ownership. The court mostly applied partition by sale to co-owned buildings. Also, the amendment of 2009 has significantly reduced the frequency of partition by sale. The court has been inclined to adopt partition by sale when partition in kind would fragment land parcels.[149]

3. Partition of Things Held in Joint and Indivisible Ownership

157. The aforementioned doctrines apply *mutatis mutandis* to joint and indivisible ownership.[150] Co-owners under joint and indivisible ownership, however, may not petition for partition for the duration of the relationship.[151]

C. Covenant to Administer Co-owned Property and Covenants Not to Partition

158. Article 826-1 stipulates that covenants to administer or use co-owned immovable things shall run with assets on the condition that they have been registered. Scholars have pointed out that Article 826-1 can be utilized as a platform to create any type of new real property right—to avoid the constraints set by the

149. Yun-chien Chang & Lee Anne Fennell, *Appendices to Partition and Revelation*, 81 U. Chicago L. Rev. Dialogue 1 (2014); Yun-chien Chang & Lee Anne Fennell, *Partition and Revelation*, 81 U. Chicago L. Rev. 27 (2014); Yun-chien Chang, *An Empirical Study of Co-Ownership Partition Cases in Taiwan: 2008–2010*, in *Empirical Studies of the Judicial Systems 2011* 221–264 (Yun-chien Chang ed., Taiwan: Institutum Iurisprudentiae, Academia Sinica 2013).
150. Taiwan Civil Code, Art. 830.
151. Taiwan Civil Code, Art. 829.

numerus clausus principle. In practice, however, co-owners very rarely register their covenants. Thus, Article 826-1, as a vehicle for creating new property forms, remains a theoretical construct.

159. Article 826-1 also allows covenants not to partition to be binding for third parties as long as they accompany covenants to manage or use the co-owned things and are registered. There is a thirty-year time limit on such covenants,[152] allowing co-owners to reconsider the most valuable use of their properties at least every thirty years.[153] Co-tenants, however, may still petition courts to partition before the agreed time limit is hit, with a significant cause.[154]

II. Co-ownership Applied to Apartment Buildings

160. The Taiwan Civil Code only contains a few articles on co-ownership applied to apartment buildings—that is, condominium form.[155] The Condominium Administration Act of Taiwan (CAA) is the major source of law. Below, regulations stipulated by administrative agencies (mainly the Ministry of the Interior) and court decisions are also drawn on.

A. A Sub-area Becomes a Field of Its Own

161. The condominium form has been recognized by law since as early as 1930 when the Taiwan Civil Code went into effect. The Taiwan Civil Code of 1930, however, contained only two articles regarding condominium form, which were insufficient to delineate the rights and duties of residents in apartment buildings.[156] In 1987, the central competent authority, the Ministry of the Interior, drafted a bill on condominium form, but the bill did not become a statute. In 1989, the Ministry of the Interior commissioned two famous scholars and a justice at the Constitutional Court to draft a new bill on condominium form. After an amendment by the legal task force at the Ministry of the Interior, the bill was sent to the Legislative Yuan, which passed the Condominium Administration Act after several revisions in 1995. To date, the Condominium Administration Act is still the major source of condominium stipulations, and the Condominium Administration Act is often described as "the constitution for residential housing."

---

152. The time limit for other covenants, such as those for co-owned movable things, is five years.
153. Taiwan Civil Code, Art. 823.
154. Taiwan Civil Code, Art. 823.
155. This section is adapted from Yun-chien Chang, *Condominium Law in Taiwan: Doctrinal Overview under the Lens of Information-Cost Theory*, 23 Asia Pacific L. Rev. 89 (2015).
156. Taiwan Civil Code, Art. 800. It was contended that the original Taiwanese Civil Code Art. 799 could only apply to real estate developments in which units were vertically separated (such as townhouses), but not those that were horizontally separated (such as apartment buildings). The Supreme Court of Taiwan has ruled in a case that Art. 799 applies to horizontally separated units. This legal uncertainty, among others, was the driving force behind a fuller-scale condominium law. *See* Taiwan Civil Code, Art. 799; *See* Zui Gao Fa Yuan 80 Nian Tai Shang Zi Di 804 Hao Pan Jue [Supreme Court 1991 No. 804 Decision].

162. Another wave of improvement in condominium law came in 2009 when the Taiwan Civil Code was amended. Taiwan Civil Code Article 799 was expanded, but the new stipulations are only a summary of the most important definitions already existent in the Condominium Administration Act.[157] The new Taiwan Civil Code Article 799-2 allows the sole owner of a building to convert it to condominium form.[158] Taiwan Civil Code Article 799-1 does some heavy lifting. Its paragraph 3 gives minority apartment owners who disagree with the amendment of their "condominium bylaw" a cause of action to petition the court to revoke any "obviously unfair" amendment within three months after the decision is made. According to its paragraph 4, condominium bylaws bind grantees of unit ownership, whether they know the contents or not. Also, other covenants among unit owners bind successors even without their actual knowledge of the covenants, whereas purchasers or the like of unit ownership are bound only if they know or should have known these covenants.

B. Threefold Relationship

163. Condominium form of shared ownership in Taiwan implicitly recognizes the "threefold relationship" (*Dreigliedrige Einheit* in German). The threefold relationship consists of private ownership of an apartment, co-ownership of the common areas,[159] and membership in the condominium association. The lawmaker explicitly defines "unit ownership" as containing only the former two elements of the threefold relationship.[160] Nonetheless, membership in the condominium association is a built-in feature of unit ownership.[161] The legislature does not conceptualize membership as part of the property rights of unit owners, but functionally Taiwan has the equivalent of the threefold relationship.

164. Between the so-called dualistic system and unitary system, the Taiwan regime better fits the description of the former, under which the private ownership of an apartment and the co-ownership of the common property are of equal importance, and together form a "composite ownership."

C. Physical Division of the Buildings and Land

165. A building held in condominium form and its base land can be further divided into components. The building contains multiple apartments and common facilities such as elevators. An apartment constitutes an individual unit,[162] whereas common facilities constitute the shared area, which is, along with base land,

157. Taiwan Civil Code, Art. 799.
158. Taiwan Civil Code, Art. 799-2.
159. To be more exact, the common areas are held in tenancy in common, but co-tenants cannot request partition of the shared area. Taiwan Civil Code, Art. 823.
160. Condominium Administration Act, Art. 3(1).
161. Condominium Administration Act, Art. 25.
162. The scope of the apartment is specified in Condominium Administration Act, Art. 56(3).

co-owned by all unit owners pro-rata. Designated shared areas are "individual units in the condominium that are designated for common use by agreement," whereas designated private areas, sometimes called "limited property," are common areas of a high- or low-rise that are designated by agreement to be used by specific unit owners.[163]

166. The responsibility for maintenance and reparation of common areas can be exemplified when an outside window is broken not through the faults of residents, but by natural forces such as strong wind. The unit owner can (but is not obliged to, unless otherwise mandated by the condominium bylaws) fix the window in his or her apartment at his or her own expenses.[164] If the window is installed in the common areas, the responsibility for reparation falls on the board, which either uses the common fund[165] or assesses a fee from all unit owners pro-rata to defray the expenses,[166] unless otherwise required by the condominium bylaws or condominium association. Nonetheless, an inhabitant breaking a window in the shared area still has to pay.[167]

167. The unit owner's share of the common areas and base land is determined by the area of her apartment divided by the total area of all apartments. For example, a unit owner's share is in principle 8% if her unit area is 800 m^2 and the total area is 10,000 m^2.[168] In the simplest case, if all apartments in a low-rise are of equal size, a unit owner's share is the inverse of the unit number (say, one-twelfth). The default quorum rule applies to both the number of unit owners and the percentages of shares.

---

163. Condominium Administration Act Art. 7 lists the inherent limitation of designated private areas: "Any of the common areas of a condominium may not be used as part of an individual unit. The items specified in the following subparagraphs may not be designated as designated private areas: 1. The lot the condominium is built on; 2. The hallways or stairs leading to a number of individual units, the passages or vestibule leading to the outdoors, and the alleys and fire escape alleys within the community; 3. The foundation, principal beams and pillars, load-bearing walls, and the structures of floors and roof of the condominium; 4. When such designation is in violation of related laws; 5. Any other common areas that have been designed for particular purposes and are indispensable in the daily activities of all the unit owners." Condominium Administration Act, Arts. 3(1), 7.
164. Condominium Administration Act, Art. 10(1).
165. The source of common fund is stipulated in Condominium Administration Act, Art. 18(1): "Each condominium shall establish a common fund from the following sources: 1. The builder of the condominium is required to provide a certain percentage of the cost of the project or a certain amount to pay for the management and maintenance during the year after the usage license is obtained; 2. Each unit owner pays an amount as decided by the community association; 3. The interest accrued on the fund; 4. Other incomes." Enforcement Rules for the Condominium Administration Act Art. 5 provides concrete percentage numbers (0.3%, 0.5%, 1.5%, or 2%) that the builder shall use to compute its assessment due to the common fund. *See* Condominium Administration Act, Arts. 5, 18(1).
166. Repairing certain facilities in the shared area may be subsidized by the government. *See* Condominium Administration Act, Art. 10(3).
167. Condominium Administration Act, Art. 10(3).
168. *See* Taiwan Civil Code, Art. 799(4); Condominium Administration Act, Art. 1.

D. Obligations of Apartment Inhabitants

168. An inhabitant has to pay assessments to the common fund usually every month and share the reparation and maintenance expenses pro-rata.[169] If inhabitants have missed paying their monthly charges or shared expenses twice and refuse to comply after being given notice to make the payment within a specified period, the manager or board may sue the inhabitants in court for the payment plus the overdue interest.[170]

169. Certain conducts are prohibited by the Condominium Administration Act or condominium bylaws. For instance, the following alterations are subject to the condominium bylaws and community association resolutions "that have been reported to the local competent authority": changing structures or colors and installing advertising signs or metal gratings on the exterior wall of the building, on the rooftop terrace, or in air raid shelters.[171] Moreover, inhabitants should not create a nuisance, such as discarding garbage or making unreasonable noise,[172] blocking or possessing fire escape alleys, open spaces, stair landings, common hallways, or air raid shelters.[173]

170. The management body can evict uncooperative inhabitants who violate certain rules. The common preconditions for eviction are: (1) Inhabitants "fail to make the improvement within 3 months after the manager or board urges for improvement" and (2) Community association makes a resolution of eviction. One of the following conditions also has to be met: first, owed expenses reach one-hundredth of the total value of the apartment; second, inhabitants make no improvement or continue to violate rules after civil fines have been imposed according to Article 49(1) of the Condominium Administration Act;[174] third, inhabitants have violated the condominium bylaws or laws to a serious extent. In practice, boards have successfully evicted inhabitants who failed to pay their monthly assessments, inhabitants who were mentally ill and threw knives at neighbors, and inhabitants who swore at and hit other inhabitants.

171. If the uncooperative inhabitant is a unit owner, the officer (or board) may petition the court for an injunction to force the unit owner to sell his or her unit ownership, again on the condition that the community association makes such a resolution. If the habitant fails to complete the transaction and finalize the ownership

169. Condominium Administration Act, Art. 18(1).
170. Condominium Administration Act, Art. 21.
171. The board can stop the act of the violator and request the violator to restore. *See* Condominium Administration Act, Art. 8(1), 8(3).
172. Condominium Administration Act, Art. 16(1).
173. If any inhabitant should create the aforementioned nuisance, "the manager or board shall stop the act or take action according to the condominium bylaws." Condominium Administration Act, Art. 16(2).
174. Condominium Administration Act Art. 49(1) penalizes a unit owner in violation of Art. 5; Art. 8, para. 1; Art. 9, para. 2; and Art. 16, paras. 2–3. It also punishes an inhabitant who changes the purposes of use of an individual unit or a designated private area. Condominium Administration Act, Art. 49(1).

transfer registration within three months after the final court decision, the officer (or board) may petition the court to put the unit ownership up for auction.[175] A comprehensive survey of the case law reveals that the officer (or board) in most lawsuits only requested evictions, not forced sales. In a few cases, the officer (or board) requested forced sales and the court agreed, because the unit owners owed their monthly assessment or changed the structure of the building—endangering public safety.[176]

E. Condominium Bylaws

172. Condominium bylaws are the constitution of apartment buildings.[177] Condominium bylaws supplement and sometimes supersede stipulations in the Condominium Administration Act and the Taiwan Civil Code. More specifically, condominium bylaws interact with statutes in the following ways: First, stipulations in the Condominium Administration Act and the Taiwan Civil Code with the phrase "unless otherwise stipulated by condominium bylaws" are clearly default rules that can be contracted around. Second, some, like Condominium Administration Act Article 7, are clearly mandatory rules that condominium bylaws cannot alter.[178] Third, certain joint decisions are effective only when incorporated in the condominium bylaw—that is, ordinary resolutions by community association on whether such matters are invalid.[179] This is to reduce information costs for current and future unit owners, as condominium bylaws are a salient document, easy to retrieve.[180] Fourth, certain condominium bylaws are valid upon reporting to,[181] or even approval by,[182] the local competent authorities. Finally, there are stipulations that can be a default rule or a mandatory rule, leaving the court more room for interpretation. Note also that a mandatory rule can be interpreted as setting a ceiling, a floor, or both, and it is not always clear from the statutes which type of mandatory rule is prescribed.

175. Condominium Administration Act, Art. 22(2).
176. *See* Chang, *supra* n. 103.
177. Condominium Administration Act, Art. 23; Taiwan Civil Code, Art. 799-1.
178. Article 7 forbids certain common areas to be used as part of an individual unit.
179. Pursuant to Condominium Administration Act Art. 23(2), these joint decisions are: "1. The range and the users of individual units and designated common areas; 2. The rights of each unit owner to use and to benefit from the common areas and the base, and the special agreements of unit owners on the use of the common areas; 3. Special agreements on prohibition of pet keeping by the inhabitants; 4. Measures for handling of obligation violations; 5. Regulations on supervision of financial management; 6. Special agreements on the required numbers and unit ownership proportions of the attending and approving unit owners to hold the community association and to approve the decisions; 7. The procedure for dispute mediation." *See* Condominium Administration Act, Art. 23(2).
180. These joint decisions are important ones that warrant careful deliberation. Given that condominium bylaws may enact different quorum rules for revising condominium bylaws and for making less important resolutions, the mandatory rule to utilize condominium bylaws to make important decisions ensures that they are made with sufficiently wide support from unit owners.
181. Condominium Administration Act, Art. 8(1).
182. Condominium Administration Act, Art. 16(2).

173. A condominium bylaw comes into being in several stages. A builder, who may or may not be the developer/constructor, should file a draft condominium bylaw when applying for the building permit.[183] The draft condominium bylaw is presumed to be the bylaw of the high- or low-rise before the official condominium bylaw is enacted.[184] It is advised that the draft condominium bylaw takes reference from the model condominium bylaw stipulated by the Ministry of the Interior.[185] When half of the units and half of the shares are already sold, the builder is obliged to convene the first community association within three months.[186] The Condominium Administration Act, however, only mandates the first community association to form a board, but does not prescribe that an official condominium bylaw has to be passed. The condominium bylaw shall then be passed according to the quorum rule prescribed by the draft condominium bylaw. Revision of the official condominium bylaw shall be done pursuant to the "$^2/_3$ + $^3/_4$" quorum rule specified in Article 31 of the Condominium Administration Act (more on this in Part XII), unless otherwise stipulated in the official condominium bylaw. It is not uncommon for common-interest communities to add substantive contents into the condominium bylaws.

174. Condominium bylaws are similar to co-ownership covenants, but they are also different in several important aspects. First, co-ownership covenants require consensus among co-tenants, while condominium bylaws can generally be passed with a super-majority vote. Second, co-ownership covenants can only stipulate the management of co-owned properties, while condominium bylaws can limit the ways unit owners utilize their own apartments. Third, condominium bylaws need not and cannot be registered in the land registry, whereas co-ownership covenants regarding immovable properties have to be registered to be valid.[187]

175. Condominium bylaws are in rem and bind all current and future unit owners, even illegal possessors,[188] without their knowledge.[189] The bylaws, thus, are clearly not just contracts, but a type of new property form. Other covenants among unit owners, including but not limited to resolutions by the community association and a bilateral agreement between two unit owners (who, say, own apartments on the same floor regarding pet and party policies), also have a third-party effect, unless the grantees of unit ownership are bona fide (i.e., not knowing) purchasers without negligence.[190]

183. Condominium Administration Act, Art. 56(1).
184. Condominium Administration Act, Art. 56(2).
185. Condominium Administration Act, Art. 60.
186. Condominium Administration Act, Art. 28.
187. Taiwan Civil Code, Art. 826(1).
188. Condominium Administration Act, Art. 24(2).
189. Taiwan Civil Code, Art. 799-1(4).
190. Taiwan Civil Code, Art. 799-1.

176. The latter stipulation (the conditional in rem effect) should be interpreted along with Condominium Administration Act Article 24, which mandates the grantees to (1) ask the manager or board for access to the documents specified in Condominium Administration Act Article 35 before the granting and (2) abide by all the obligations of the original unit owner defined in the Condominium Administration Act or the condominium bylaws. The documents specified in Article 35 include:

- condominium bylaws;
- the spreadsheet of the common fund;
- the accounting vouchers;
- the account books;
- the financial reports;
- the outstanding payments of common fund, shared expenses, and other payable expenses of the inhabitants;
- the board meeting minutes;
- the unit assembly meeting minutes.

177. Taken together, grantees are bound by other covenants among unit owners when the covenants are chronicled in one of the two meeting minutes and are on file with the manager or the board, whether grantees have asked for them or not because grantees should have had access to them and would have known. By contrast, grantees are not bound if: 1) they ask the board for the documents, 2) the covenants in question cannot be found in the provided documents, and 3) it is unreasonable for grantees to find the loopholes themselves. In addition, covenants made by a limited number of unit owners will probably not be included in the meeting minutes. If a grantor failed to inform her grantee, in general (but still depending on context) it is difficult for grantees to ascertain the existence of such covenants.

178. The courts in Taiwan have held in several cases that grantees who know, or should have known, the contents of the covenants be bound. In a case involving presale apartments, the covenant between the developer and all the purchasers prescribed that the basement counts as an individual unit and belongs to the developer, who then voluntarily provided the basement as a shared area for installing water and electrical facilities. The court ruled that the party who purchased the basement later from the developer should be bound by the covenant, as the facilities were easy to find.[191] In a case with a similar arrangement of the basement, the court ruled that the owners who acquired the basement in court auctions should still be bound.[192] In one case, a newcomer challenged the arrangement of designated private areas, but

191. Tai Wan Gao Deng Fa Yuan Tai Nan Fen Yuan 102 Nian Du Shang Yi Zi Di 21 Hao Min Shi Pan Jue [High Court 2013 No. 21 Decision].
192. Tai Wan Shi Lin Di Fang Fa Yuan 101 Nian Du Su Zi Di 111 Hao Min Shi Pan Jue [District Court 2012 Appeal No. 111 Decision].

the court ruled that this arrangement was easy to observe.[193] In two cases, new residents challenged the arrangement of designated shared areas, and the courts again ruled against the plaintiff for similar reasons—because the arrangements were obvious.[194]

F. Parking Space

179. Parking spaces may be located in any of the four units or areas described above, and the legal arrangements for them are one of the more complex problems in condominium law in Taiwan.[195] The Condominium Administration Act does not clearly delineate the rights of parking spaces[196]—perhaps one of the major reasons that parking rights are a mess. There are three types of parking spaces: statutory parking spaces（法定停車位）, reward parking spaces（獎勵增設停車位）, and additional parking spaces（自行增設停車位）. They are introduced in turn below.

180. Statutory parking spaces are mandated by statutes (Article 58 of the Condominium Administration Act). They are located in the common areas of buildings or the base land. Their exclusive use right（專用權）can only be acquired, according to the stipulations in condominium bylaws, by a unit owner (Article 58(2) of the Condominium Administration Act).[197]

181. Reward parking spaces are not mandated by the Condominium Administration Act, but are created by an incentive-based regulation that encourages developers to create parking spaces for the general public (including the inhabitants[198]) in exchange for higher floor-area ratios（容積率）. They are usually located on a separate floor of the building. The separate floor as a whole is an "individual unit"

---

193. Tai Wan Tai Bei Di Fang Fa Yuan 100 Nian Du Su Zi Di 3156 Hao Min Shi Pan Jue [District Court 2011 Appeal No. 3156 Decision].
194. Tai Wan Gao Xiong Di Fang Fa Yuan 101 Nian Du Jian Shang Zi Di 281 Hao Min Shi Pan Jue [District Court 2012 No.281 Decision]; Tai Wan Gao Xiong Di Fang Fa Yuan 100 Nian Du Feng Jian Zi Di 721 Hao Min Shi Pan Jue [District Court 2011 No. 721 Decision].
195. For an overview of this problem, *see* Tsay-chuan Hsieh, 1 *Property Law* 388–392 (Author 5th ed. 2010); Chia-Pei Chan, *Legal Issues of Parking Space in Apartment Buildings* (Jun. 21, 2013) (unpublished Master's thesis, Chung Cheng University).
196. Only CAA, s. 58 touches upon the issue, stipulating that "[t]he builder or construction company of the condominium may not sell any part of common areas, including statutory open space, statutory parking spaces and statutory air raid shelter facilities to specific individuals or register any specific individuals outside the unit owners for the right of designated private usages or do anything that will jeopardize the interests of the unit owners."
197. As statutory parking space is co-owned by all unit owners, scholars have criticized the fact that developers (not being owners) can sell the exclusive rights of statutory parking space to certain unit owners. Sales of these parking rights are often stipulated in the draft condominium bylaws and it is included in the apartment sale contract as an appendix, thus binding all purchasers. *See* Feng-Wen Wen, *On Certain Problems of Condo Administrative Act,* 140 Taiwan L. J. 1, 4 (2009). Scholars thus have advocated that the exclusive use rights of parking space should be left to the community association to allocate and manage. *Ibid.*, 7.
198. An inhabitant（住戶）refers to a unit owner, a tenant, an individual using a unit with the approval of the owner, or an individual having acquired the ownership of a parking space in the building (Condominium Administration Act, Art. 3(1)).

and is held as unit ownership. A floor contains multiple parking spaces, the exclusive use rights of which can be acquired through "co-ownership covenants"[199] (分管契約; Article 826-1 of the Taiwan Civil Code).

182. In addition to the statutory parking spaces, extra parking spaces are voluntarily constructed by developers, in the high- or low-rise or its surrounding land, without the bonus floor-area ratio. If this type of parking space is located on a separate floor of the building, the arrangement is similar to that of reward parking spaces. However, if the statutory parking spaces and the additional parking spaces are located on the same floor, the exclusive use right for additional parking space can only be acquired by a unit owner, according to the stipulations in condominium bylaws—like the right of statutory parking space.

183. The arrangement of exclusive use rights of parking space,[200] if appropriately handled, can bind future grantees of ownership of units in the apartment building. The use rights stipulated in the condominium bylaws are in rem and bind third parties, in good faith or bad faith (Article 799-1(4) of the Taiwan Civil Code and Article 24(1) of the Condominium Administration Act). The arrangement stipulated in co-ownership covenants can bind grantees if registered in the land registry.[201]

G. Community Association

184. The community association shall convene according to the following procedures. The assembly must be held at least once a year,[202] initiated by the chairperson of the board,[203] who issues a written ten-day notice (that carries the agenda) to each unit owner.[204] An ad hoc assembly may convene if an announcement is

---

199. For an economic analysis of co-ownership covenant, *see* Yun-chien Chang & Henry E. Smith, *An Economic Analysis of Civil versus Common Law Property*, 88 Notre Dame L. R. 1, 45–46 (2012).
200. For arguments that use rights of parking spaces are closer to licensing and assignment of intellectual property rights, *see* Ming-Cheng Tsai, *Shares of Basement Ownership and Co-ownership Covenant of Parking Space*, 18 Court Case Times 90, 95 (2012).
201. Regarding parking space arrangement as co-ownership covenant, *see* Ming-Cheng Tsai, *Individual Units in Apartment Buildings and Co-ownership Covenants*, 13 Court Case Times 28, 31 (2012).
202. Condominium Administration Act, Art. 25(1).
203. Condominium Administration Act, Art. 3.
204. Condominium Administration Act, Art. 30(1). Condominium Administration Act Arts. 25(3) and 25(4) stipulate detailed procedures for convening the community association when there is no chairperson of the board: '3. … When there is no manager or board or when the manager, or chairperson or members of the board are not unit owners, the unit owners shall elect among them a person to be the convener. The term of convener is one to two years as set forth in the condominium bylaws or determined by the community association. The convener may serve a second term when reelected. If neither the condominium bylaws nor the community association has made any specification, the term shall be one year and the convener may serve a second term when reelected. 4. When the convener cannot be elected according to the regulation as prescribed in the preceding paragraph, the unit owners may apply to the competent authority of the special municipality or county/city for appointing a temporary convener. If the unit owners have not made the application,

posted at least two days in advance[205] and if one of the following conditions holds: (1) "when critical incidents that require timely handling have taken place and the manager or board has made the request to convene the assembly" or (2) "over one-fifth of the unit owners who own more than one-fifth of the shares request to convene the community association."[206]

185. The Condominium Administration Act designs a default quorum rule for both the ordinary and exceptional procedures for convening the community association and voting. All resolutions (including those revising condominium bylaws) made by the community association require (1) the attendance of at least two-thirds of the unit owners who also represent at least two-thirds of the shares[207] and (2) the consent of at least three-quarters of the attendees who represent at least three-quarters of the shares.[208] When a decision cannot be made according to the aforementioned "$^2/_3 + {}^3/_4$ rule," the convener of community association may convene another meeting to decide on the same issue. Under such circumstances, unless otherwise stipulated in the condominium bylaws, the "$^1/_5 + {}^1/_2$ rule" is adopted instead.[209] Unit owners who are unable to attend a community association may delegate in writing to one of the following persons to attend: his or her spouse, parents, or adult children; another unit owner or a tenant of any unit.[210] No unit owner may control more than one-fifth of the total possible votes, either through representing his or her own multiple units or as a proxy voter for others.[211] The aforementioned default rule can be changed by condominium bylaws. Two concrete alternatives are provided by the model condominium bylaw.

186. As for minority protection, the opposing unit owners may file a claim with the court to revoke the condominium bylaw within three months of its revision or establishment.[212] A few district courts applied the Taiwan Civil Code Article 799-1(3) to revoke the revisions to the condominium bylaws because the community association had singled out one or a minority of unit owners and increased their parking fee or monthly assessments, which was unfair, unreasonable, or discriminatory.[213] A gap in the law is whether the court may revoke resolutions by community association that do not amend the condominium bylaw. There was a case in

---

the competent authority of the special municipality or county/city may appoint a unit owner to be the temporary convener or the unit owners may rotate as the convener according to the condominium bylaws until the unit owners have elected a convener from among them'. *See* Condominium Administration Act, Art. 25(3), 25(4).

205. Condominium Administration Act, Art. 30(1).
206. Condominium Administration Act, Art. 25(2).
207. One individual unit, one vote. A co-owned individual unit has one vote, cast by the representative selected by the co-owners. *See* Condominium Administration Act, Art. 27(1).
208. Condominium Administration Act, Art. 31.
209. Condominium Administration Act, Art. 32.
210. Condominium Administration Act, Art. 27(3).
211. Condominium Administration Act, Art. 27(2), 27(3).
212. Taiwan Civil Code, Art. 799-1(3).
213. Tai Wan Gao Xiong Di Fang Fa Yuan 102 Nian Du Su Zi Di 1891 Hao Min Shi Pan Jue [District Court 2013 Appeal No. 1891 Decision]; Tai Wan Xin Bei Di Fang Fa Yuan 102 Nian Du Su Zi Di

which both the district court and the appellate court applied the Taiwan Civil Code Article 799-1(3) *mutatis mutandis* to revoke such a resolution.[214]

187. Lease tenants have limited capacity to get involved in the management of apartment building affairs. Community association is, by definition, a meeting of all unit owners. Tenants do not have a right to vote, other than by serving as a proxy voter.[215] The Condominium Administration Act is silent as to whether tenants have the right to participate and speak in the community association. A tenant can serve as a member or chairperson of the board, unless the condominium bylaw or community association stipulates otherwise.[216]

§2. CONCURRENT OWNERSHIP OF MOVABLE PROPERTY

188. All the stipulations described above in §1 apply to both immovable and movable properties. The sole exception is the rule regarding covenants to manage co-owned movable properties. Such covenants run to transferees of movable properties if the transferees know or should have known the covenants.[217]

1416 Hao Min Shi Pan Jue [District Court 2013 Appeal No. 1416 Decision]; Tai Wan Gao Xiong Di Fang Fa Yuan 99 Nian Du Xiong Jian Zi Di 2056 Hao Min Shi Pan Jue [District Court 2010 No. 2056 Decision].

214. Tai Wan Gao Deng Fa Yuan Tai Nan Fen Yuan 100 Nian Du Shang Zi Di 250 Hao Min Shi Pan Jue [High Court 2011 No. 250 Decision]; Tai Wan Tai Nan Di Fang Fa Yuan 99 Nian Du Su Zi Di 1672 Hao Min Shi Pan Jue [District Court 2010 No. 1672 Decision]. In this case, the community association singles out the plaintiff and unreasonably increases its monthly assessment.

215. Condominium Administration Act, Arts. 25, 27.

216. Condominium Administration Act, Art. 29(5).

217. This rule is derived from Judicial Yuan Interpretation No. 349. *See* Taiwan Civil Code, Art. 826-1.

Chapter 7. Neighborhood and Urban Problems

189. This chapter covers the stipulations in the Taiwan Civil Code that are often collectively called the "neighbour relation law." A majority of Taiwanese live in urban areas, and many of them live in apartment buildings. Condominium law, while practically highly important, will be covered in Chapter 6 of Part I.

§1. Legal Servitude of Passage

190. In the Taiwan Civil Code, six articles stipulate legal servitude of passage.[218,219] Four of them address the access problem for landlocked land, whereas the other two deal with drainage work that has to pass through adjacent land and "incidental actions" by the owner of the dominant land. Landlocked land is defined as a land parcel lacking "suitable access"[220] to a public road and as a result, can be used ordinarily.[221] A legal servitude is "legal" in the sense that it is prescribed by law. There are two types of legal servitude of passage: statutory easement and easement of necessity, which are introduced below.

I. Statutory Easement

A. Necessity

191. A statutory right of way is granted to landlocked owners to pass through neighboring land. The passage has to be necessary.[222] In court practice, a necessary access is context-dependent. Sometimes it means "wide enough for sedans," whereas sometimes it means "wide enough for certain machines or trucks." In a majority of cases, the width of the passage is smaller than or equal to four meters.[223]

192. The landlocked owners may have the right to construct a road (instead of merely passing) if necessary. If the servient land suffers from excessive damage as a result, the servient landowner may require the dominant landowner to purchase

---

218. Taiwan Civil Code, Arts. 779, 786–789, 854.
219. For an economic analysis of this doctrine, *see* Yun-chien Chang, *Hybrid Rule: Hidden Entitlement Protection Rule in Access to Landlocked Land Doctrine*, 91 Tulane Law Review 217 (2016).
220. In court practice, connecting roads that are too narrow or too steep have been considered unsuitable accesses. *See* Yun-chien Chang, *An Empirical Study of Legal Servitude of Passage Cases in Taiwan,* 216 Taiwan L. R. 211, 211–227 (2013).
221. Taiwan Civil Code, Art. 787.
222. Taiwan Civil Code, Art. 787.
223. Yun-chien Chang, *An Empirical Study of Legal Servitude of Passage Cases in Taiwan,* 216 Taiwan L. R. 211, 211–227 (2013).

the land accessed and the subsequently created odd lot for a reasonable price. If the parties cannot agree upon the purchase price, the price shall be determined by a court.[224]

B. Voluntary Act Exception

193. Land becomes landlocked for several possible reasons: voluntary acts of landowners themselves (such as severance), third-party actions (such as building a highway, a golf course, or new houses in surrounded plots), abolishment of public roads by the government, and acts of God (such as an earthquake or tsunami). The statutory easement law deals with land becoming landlocked due to the last three reasons, whereas the easement of necessity law handles land that loses its usual access because of the first reason. More precisely, there are two types of voluntary acts: one is a landowner's decision to block or ruin an existing passage; the other is the (co-)owners' decision to partition or partially transfer land and leave part of the land parcel landlocked. No easements will be prescribed following the first type of voluntary act,[225] because otherwise, landowners have incentive to cut their existing routes through their own land and seek legal servitude of passage over their neighbors' plots instead.

C. Passage Location: The Least Damage Rule

194. The location of a right of way shall be set at the place that "causes the least damage to the adjacent plot."[226] Many district court cases have elaborated the least damage rule, but the interpretations are again fact-driven and context-dependent. No abstract rule emerges from those cases. More specifically, a majority of cases considered the length, width, and area of the passage, whereas only a few cases took into account the land value of the passage.[227]

D. Compensation

195. Landlocked owners are required to compensate owners of neighboring parcels.[228] The compensation in court practice is not calculated based on fair market value; rather, it is assessed based on Declared Land Value, a value that, in the case of private land, is almost always 80% of Public Land Value (aka Publicly Announced Land Value), a land value announced by local government for tax purposes every three years. Public Land Value has been less than 50% of fair market

224. Taiwan Civil Code, Art. 788.
225. Taiwan Civil Code, Art. 787.
226. *Ibid.*
227. Yun-chien Chang, *An Empirical Study of Legal Servitude of Passage Cases in Taiwan,* 216 Taiwan L. R. 221, 211–227 (2013).
228. Taiwan Civil Code, Art. 787.

value for decades.[229] The annual land yield rate used in the computation has been found to be determined quite arbitrarily. As a whole, the court-adjudicated compensation is below market rent.

II. Easement of Necessity

196. Easement of necessity is also called "easements by necessity" or "ways of necessity." If, as a result of a partition or a partial transfer, a land parcel becomes landlocked, its owner is implied by law to have an easement over a neighboring parcel which was originally part of the co-owned land (in the case of partition) or was separated from the landlocked parcel because of a previous partial transfer. Namely, the easement of necessity doctrine puts restrictions on the landlocked owners' choice of servient land. Landlocked owners can only pass through land parcels owned by a former co-owner (or his or her transferee) or land parcels that have been part of the same plots with the landlocked parcels. This rule bars externalization of passage costs and induces owners of potential landlocked land and servient land to arrange for passage before any land becomes landlocked. A co-tenant partitioning the co-owned land parcel (or an owner transferring part of his or her land) is able to avoid creating landlocked parcels by planning for the right of passage when partitioning or transferring. For example, co-tenants may keep a lengthy plot co-owned and use it as a passage, or the transferor can structure a voluntary right of way between the potentially landlocked parcel and the servient, neighboring parcel.

197. Moreover, the passage has to be furnished gratuitously.[230]

§2. Building Encroachment

198. The entitlement of the neighbor (whose land is trespassed) is generally protected when the encroachment[231] is intentional or grossly negligent. That is, the neighbor can request the encroaching buildings be removed. The entitlement, however, is only partially protected if the neighbor fails to promptly protest to the negligent trespasser of his or her disapproval upon being aware of the trespass. Without protesting promptly, the neighbor cannot request removal, but can only request that the encroacher purchase "the part of the trespassed land" and "the odd lot caused by the trespass" at a "reasonable price." Alternatively, the neighbor can request payment for his or her losses.[232]

---

229. Yun-chien Chang, *Empire Building and Fiscal Illusion? An Empirical Study of Government Official Behaviors in Takings*, 6 J. Empirical Legal Stud. 541 (2009); Yun-chien Chang, *Private Property and Takings Compensation: Theoretical Framework and Empirical Analysis* (Edward Elgar 2013).

230. Taiwan Civil Code, Art. 789.

231. Adapted from Yun-chien Chang, The Evolution of Property Law in Taiwan: An Unconventional Interest Group Story, in *Private Law in China and Taiwan: Economic and Legal Anaylses* (eds Yun-chien Chang et al., Cambridge Univ. Press 2016).

232. Taiwan Civil Code, Art. 796.

199. If the trespass is unintentional, the court, after taking into account "the public interests and the interests of the two parties," may order preservation rather than removal.[233]

200. The building encroachment doctrine applies to residential buildings and applies *mutatis mutandis* to other types of construction that are "similarly valuable."[234] Surveys of court cases reveal that the encroaching constructions were mostly residential and non-residential buildings, rather than fixtures like fences or extensions like garages. Note that if the encroaching part and non-encroaching part of the building are separate—the test developed by courts being "tearing down the encroaching part would not affect 'the economic value of the whole building'"—courts would order the encroaching part removed.[235]

I. The Prompt Protest Rule

201. The prompt protest rule applies when the encroachers are not grossly negligent. In Taiwan, most encroachers nowadays are grossly negligent. Verifying real estate information (including boundaries) in the registry has become extremely easy in Taiwan, and an official survey, which is generally required before a developer applies for a building permit, is inexpensive (less than USD 150 for most landowners) and definitive in setting land boundaries.

202. Encroachers have the burden of proof as to whether their neighbors have failed to promptly protest. In practice, encroachers have rarely met this burden of proof.

II. Mandatory Purchase and Compensation

203. In practice, neighbors rarely request that encroachers purchase "the part of the trespassed land" and "the odd lot caused by the trespass" at a "reasonable price,"[236] because courts use Declared Land Value, which is far below fair market value, to determine the price, and people bargain in the shadow of law.

204. Like in legal servitude of passage cases, courts in building encroachment cases also use Declared Land Value and ad hoc determined land yield rates to calculate compensation for building encroachment. As a result, the compensation is below market standard.

233. Taiwan Civil Code, Art. 796-1.
234. Taiwan Civil Code, Art. 796-2.
235. Yun-chien Chang, *An Empirical Study of Boundary Encroachment Litigation,* 14 Academia Sinica L.J. 319, 319–373 (2014).
236. Taiwan Civil Code, Art. 796.

III. Discretionary Power to Remove or Preserve

205. The wide discretion of the courts in determining whether to tear down the encroaching buildings was added to the Taiwan Civil Code in 2009.[237] How did courts consider "public interests and private interests"? An empirical study shows that from 2009 (when Article 796-1 became effective) to 2020, among the 348 district court cases, 80% drew on Article 796-1 and still ordered removal, and a small area of encroachment is the best predictor for courts' ordering preservation.[238]

IV. Encroaching Plants

206. Article 797 of the Taiwan Civil Code deals with encroaching plants. It prescribes that "if the branches or roots of plants of the adjacent land have spread beyond the boundary, the landowner is entitled to require the owner of the plants to cut and rid the said branches or roots within a reasonable period. If the owner of the plants does not cut and rid the said branches or roots within the period specified in the preceding paragraph, the landowner is entitled to cut and take the encroaching branches or roots, and is also entitled to claim the expenses caused thereby. The provisions of the preceding two paragraphs shall not apply to such encroaching branches or roots that do not interfere with the utility of the land."

V. Fallen Fruits and Boundary

207. While roots and branches are considered undesirable for the encroached land and its owner, fruits are considered gifts from above. "Fruits that fall naturally on adjacent land are deemed to belong to the owner of such land, except if it is a land for public use."[239]

§3. Nuisance

208. Several articles in the Taiwan Civil Code can be aptly categorized as "nuisance law," though it is not a civil-law concept. Property right holders[240] can petition courts for injunctions against persons who create a nuisance. More specifically, property right holders have the right to not be disturbed by "the discharge of gases, steam, odours, smoke, heat, soot, noises, vibrations and the like."[241] The proviso of

---

237. Taiwan Civil Code, Art. 796-1.
238. Yun-chien Chang, *Demolish or Not? An Empirical Study of Building Encroachment Cases in 2009–2020*, 103 Court Case Times 84 (2021); Yun-chien Chang, To Tear Down or Not to Tear Down? An Empirical Study of Boundary Encroachment Cases in Taiwan, in *Empirical Legal Analysis: Assessing the Performance of Legal Institutions* 144–158 (ed. Yun-chien Chang, Routledge 2014).
239. Taiwan Civil Code, Art. 798.
240. Taiwan Civil Code, Art. 800-1.
241. Taiwan Civil Code, Art. 793.

the Taiwan Civil Code Article 793 is a "live and let live" rule, which exempts the liability of the complained person if the interference is minor or commensurate with local custom. In addition, landowners who excavate land or construct buildings should not endanger the buildings on the adjacent land.[242] Moreover, owners of adjacent land can request neighbors to undertake necessary measures to prevent their buildings from falling.[243]

§4. Legal License and Profit Rights

209. Although license and profit are common-law types of property rights, civil-property-law scholars, in general, do not conceptualize property rights in this way. Several stipulations in the Taiwan Civil Code can be considered examples of licenses and profits. The mandated licenses and profits that define what a good neighbor is are as follows. A landowner cannot evict others when they "according to the local custom, are allowed to enter unfenced field, pasture or forest for the purpose of cutting and taking grass, gathering dead branches or timber, collecting wild products, or grazing stock."[244] Possessors or owners of stray animals and lost goods are entitled to enter others' land to fetch their belongings. Landowners who tolerate the entrance can request compensation for the caused harm and can retain the goods or animals before receiving the compensation.[245] Similarly, "a landowner shall allow the owner of an adjacent plot to use his land if it is necessary for the construction or repairment of a building standing near the boundary."

§5. Water Law

210. The Taiwan Civil Code has 11 articles (775–785) on water law. The basic principle is similar to the other neighbor-relation stipulations introduced above. Nevertheless, the Water Act has superseded much of the stipulations in the Taiwan Civil Code and lays out a regulatory system of its own. These articles, therefore, are rarely used in court practice. Their contents are thus skipped.

242. Taiwan Civil Code, Art. 794.
243. Taiwan Civil Code, Art. 795.
244. Taiwan Civil Code, Art. 790.
245. Taiwan Civil Code, Art. 791.

Chapter 8. Agrarian Problems

211. Taiwan is a small country with a centralized legal system. Agrarian problems are dealt with in public law, not in property law. None of the three authors of this monograph, as private law scholars, are capable of providing an apt overview. Water Act (revised as of May 2016) governs agrarian problems. The Water Resource Agency under the Ministry of Economic Affairs is in charge of the relevant regulations. It's English website: http://eng.wra.gov.tw/ contains useful information and links for readers who are interested in this topic.

Part II. Movable Property and Personal Property/Chattels

Chapter 1. General Classification

212. The scope of personal properties in Taiwan is much narrower than that in the common law. There are no such concepts as chose in action, choses in possession, and chattel real. Funds and IP are not personal properties. The object of property rights is tangible (or corporeal) things, with pledge over rights as the only exception. The Taiwan Civil Code distinguishes between immovable properties and movable properties. Personal properties and chattels, in the Taiwan context, are coterminous with movable properties.

Chapter 2. Legal Interests

213. There is no distinction between legal and equitable interests in Taiwanese property law. The concepts of ownership and possession are not the same as those in real property law. The relationship between ownership and possession is explained in more detail in the Introduction and Chapter 3 of Part III.

214. In the Taiwan Civil Code, the section on ownership of movable properties[246] covers good-faith purchase, first possession, finders keepers, and the accession principle. They are explained in Chapters 3 and 4 of Part III.

246. Taiwan Civil Code, Arts. 801–816.

Chapter 3. Equitable Interests

215. There is no distinction between legal and equitable interests in Taiwanese property law.

Chapter 4. Security Interests (*See Also* Part VI)

216. Security interests, called security rights in this monograph to better fit Taiwan's civil-law tradition, are covered in other parts of this monograph. *See* mainly Part V.

Part III. Acquisition of Property Rights

Chapter 1. Transfer of Property by Contract Inter Vivos

§1. Introduction

217. Broadly speaking, the TCC provides for three kinds of property rights: ownership, use rights, and security rights. The subject-matter of ownership and use rights must be a tangible thing. However, while ownership can exist over movable things and immovable things, only the latter can be the subject matter of use rights. The third type of property right, i.e., security rights, is the most inclusive, because it can encompass both tangible and intangible things: movable and immovable things and rights (i.e., a creditor's right). The mode of acquiring property rights varies according to the subject matter of the relevant property right. In other words, what is important concerning the mode of acquisition of a property right is *the nature of the thing to which the property right attaches*, rather than the kind of property right itself. For reasons of space, the section introduces three things on which property rights can be engrafted: "chattels," "land" and "a creditor's right." Since the nature of each of them is different, the mode of acquiring property rights over each of them is thenceforth dissimilar, to which now we turn.

§2. Acquisition of Property Rights in Chattels (Movable/Tangible Things)

218. Chattels are movable as well as tangible things. If A wants to acquire a property right (i.e., ownership or pledge) over a chattel owned by B, what legal processes are to be satisfied in order for A to procure a property right in respect of B's chattel? In other words, what mode needs to be followed in respect of chattel transactions? Two steps are in principle required. First, there must be mutual consents between A and B on A's acquisition of a proprietary interest (ownership or pledge) in B's chattel. This involves B's intention to dispose of his property interest over the thing to A and A's intention to accept it from B. This step is commonly known as "real agreement (*dingliche Einigung*)." However, this real agreement alone cannot perfect the transaction between A and B. The second step requires delivery; *scilicet*, A and B's real agreement must be accompanied with transfer of the possession from B to A in order for a property right to be vested in A. In our example, this means that A must acquire possession of the thing from B, otherwise, acquisition of a property right on the part of A would not be effectuated. These two steps are enshrined in Article 761 of the Taiwan Civil Code as follows: "The transfer of property right in chattels will not take effect unless the thing is delivered." The "transfer" here is interpreted as being based on the parties' real agreement, and the expression "the thing is delivered" denotes that the thing in question should be possessed by the other party. To sum up, if one wants to acquire a proprietary interest in chattels via agreement, the aforementioned two steps must be met: *parties' real agreement* and *transfer of possession.*

219. An exception to the above principle merits mentioning: the case of a mortgage[247] over chattels. The mortgage over chattels[248] is a kind of security property right over chattels, which does not require that possession be held by the security right holder. In other words, a mortgage is now made to the aforementioned second step: transfer of possession is exempted. Thus, the creation of a mortgage itself does not require the creditor to obtain possession of the chattel. However, this results in the right itself being invisible, thus causing potential harm to the bona fide purchasers in the market. The law needs to strike a balance: the requirement of transfer of possession is now substituted for registration of mortgage in the public registration system.[249] Therefore, if the holder of a mortgage wants to enjoy priority over every bona fide purchaser in the market, the mortgage should be registered in the public registration system.[250] This mechanism provides debtors with great convenience, for it allows them to keep utilizing their chattels subject to the security. Yet potential disponees in the market are better protected from any unexpected damage, for they are capable of knowing the provenance of a security right held by the creditors. It should be noted that this is not the only alteration. A further condition is imposed upon the first step: the parties' real agreement should be made with a written document.[251] The upshot is that, if one wants to acquire a proprietary interest such as mortgage via agreement, the two-step structure, though modified in respect of both steps, still remains good: there must be parties' (i.e., debtor and creditor) *written* real agreement and *registration* of the property right.

---

247. The charge over chattels is regulated by the Chattels Security Transactions Act. The official translation of the title of the Act released by Taiwan's Ministry of Justice is "Personal Property Secured Transactions Act" (*see* http://law.moj.gov.tw). However, this is misleading, for the Act applies only to movable and "tangible" property (i.e., chattels), while the term "personal property" encompasses intangible property as well (i.e., intellectual property, debt, etc.). Therefore, the term "chattel(s)" is instead adopted in this work, and the name of the Act is likewise modified as follows: Chattels Security Transactions Act (hereafter, Chattels Security Transactions Act).

248. The official translation of the Act uses the term "mortgage of personal property" (please *see* http://law.moj.gov.tw). But this is hardly correct. Technically speaking, the term "mortgage," according to English law, requires the ownership of a thing be transferred to the mortgagee (i.e., creditor), but the Act does not require it: the creditor *only obtains a security right* without any ownership title being vested in him. Furthermore, the term "personal property" is, for the same reason stated in the previous footnote, not an accurate term of art to be used in this context either. However, this book still adopts the term "mortgage" used by the official translation.

249. For more details, *see* Yun-chien Chang, *Structure and Style of Property Law: The Case of Mortgage and Chattel Mortgage*, 241 Taiwan L. Rev. 77 (2015).

250. Chattels Security Transactions Act, Art. 5(1).

251. *Ibid.*

§3. Acquisition of Property Rights in Land (Immovable/Tangible Things)

220. When one wants to acquire a proprietary right in land (such as ownership), the position of the TCC is aligned with the aforementioned two-step structure applied to the case of chattel mortgages: parties' written real agreement and registration of the relevant property right. The rules are provided for in sections (1) and (2) of Article 758 respectively: "The acquisition, creation, loss or alternation of property rights in land through the juridical act are not valid unless the registration of it is made (section (1) of art. 758); The juridical act prescribed in the preceding section shall be made in writing (section (2) of art. 758)." The juridical act mentioned in both sections of the article denotes the parties' real agreement, and the law demands it be made in writing, followed by a registration. To conclude, if one wants to acquire property rights in land via agreement, the two-step structure is still maintained: there must be parties' *written* real agreement and *registration* of the relevant property right.

§4. Acquisition of Property Rights in Rights (Movable/Intangible Things)

221. An archetypal example of an acquisition of a property right in a movable, yet intangible, thing is the creditor's (e.g., A) security right imposed upon his debtor's (B) credit against another (C, who is B's debtor). This is, quite oddly, called a "pledge over rights." The subject-matter of it is not confined to credit; it also involves intellectual property rights. The section intends to focus on the former, for it is expressly provided for in the TCC, and references to the latter should be made to specialist books. So, when one wants to acquire a security property right in a credit held by a debtor against another, what legal requirements must be satisfied? The two-step process holds, yet with some modification to the second step. First, there must be parties' *written* real agreement regarding the acquisition of the security property right (i.e., the pledge over rights) on the party of the creditor.[252] However, transfer of possession and registration of the right are impossible, for credits cannot be physically possessed and the notary system for the security right over credits is not yet established in this nation. Therefore, the law offers a third route: either the creditor (A) or the debtor (B) has to *give notice* of the creation of the security right to the latter's debtor (C).[253] Otherwise, the security right over the credit does not hold good against C. Therefore, the requirements for acquisition of property rights in a right, as in the case of pledge over the debtor's credit against another, are twofold: there must be parties' *written* real agreement and *notice* of the relevant property right to the debtor.

252. Article 904 (1) of the TCC.
253. Articles 902 and 297(1) of the TCC.

Chapter 2. Transfer of Property by Death

222. The International Encyclopedia of Law (IEL) has another series of books about family and succession law. Thus, this chapter only outlines the contour of transfer of property by death.

§1. General Principle

223. The basic principle of succession is that an heir assumes all the rights and duties pertaining to the estate of the decedent at the instant the decedent dies, except those rights and duties which exclusively belong to the decedent.[254] In other words, ownership of things transfers from decedents to heirs immediately.[255] There is no probate process as it is known in common-law jurisdictions. (The estate handling procedure and its effect are stipulated in the Taiwan Civil Code.[256]) An heir's duty to repay debts of decedents, however, is limited to the value of the inherited assets. For instance, if a decedent left TWD 100 in cash, TWD 50 worth of chattels, and TWD 200 in debt, the heir is only liable to the creditor for TWD 150.[257] When there are several heirs, the whole estate is, before its partition,[258] owned in joint and indivisible ownership by the heirs.[259] For more information regarding joint and indivisible ownership, *see* Chapter 6 of Part I.

§2. Waiver of Inheritance Rights

224. An heir may waive his or her right to inheritance by filing a written declaration to courts within three months after becoming aware of his or her right to inheritance.[260] Waiver of inheritance takes effect retroactively.[261] Articles 1176 and 1176-1 of the Taiwan Civil Code prescribe the details of such waivers. The social norm was that female heirs would waive their rights of inheritance. A recent empirical study shows that while the preference for male successors still exist, female successors still receive some portion of the estate.[262]

254. Taiwan Civil Code, Art. 1148.
255. Taiwan Civil Code, Art. 1147.
256. Taiwan Civil Code, Arts. 1156–1163.
257. Taiwan Civil Code, Art. 1148.
258. Taiwan Civil Code, Art. 824; Taiwan Civil Code Arts. 1164–1173.
259. Taiwan Civil Code, Arts. 827–830.
260. Taiwan Civil Code, Art. 1174.
261. Taiwan Civil Code, Art. 1175.
262. Sieh-chuen Huang, Yun-chien Chang, and Su-Li Her, "Discrimination in Afterlife? An Empirical Study on Gender Preference in Distributing Estates by Will", *Academia Sinica Law Journal* (2023 forthcoming).

§3. Will

225. A testator may freely dispose of his or her property by a will so far as it does not contravene the provisions regarding mandatory shares.[263] Articles 1189–1198 of the Taiwan Civil Code prescribe several ways to make a will, whereas Articles 1199–1222 of the Taiwan Civil Code stipulate the effect and administration of wills.

§4. Transfer of Real Property at and after Death

226. As discussed in Chapter 2 of Part I, legal transfers of real property rights are not effective before registration in the land registry.[264] Nonetheless, an heir who acquires property rights by succession becomes the legal owner before registration, but can convey his or her property right only after registering it.[265]

---

263. Taiwan Civil Code, Arts. 1144, 1187, 1223–1225.
264. Taiwan Civil Code, Art. 758.
265. Taiwan Civil Code, Art. 759.

Chapter 3. Possession

§1. General Concept of Possession

I. Definitions

227. In civil-law countries, the difference between ownership and possession[266] is highlighted—ever since Roman law—while in the common law, this distinction is not a crucial feature.[267] Before an explanation of how possession leads to acquisition of ownership, a tour of the general concept of possession in the Taiwan Civil Code is warranted.

228. Possession means having actual control,[268] and thus possession is a fact, not a right. Scholars in Taiwan have debated whether possessors have to hold a specific "intent to possess." Despite the clear text to the contrary, many property scholars prefer a narrower definition of possession, with *animus domini* (intent to be owners) as one necessary element.

229. A person who has mere custody is "an agent in possession," who is not a possessor. In other words, an agent in possession is a person who exercises actual control over a thing for another person in the latter's household, in the latter's trade or business, or in a similar relationship, and has to follow instructions from the latter.[269] Therefore, not all persons with actual control are possessors.

230. Indirect possession is recognized as possession. In other words, "if a person possesses a thing of another as a *superficiary*, agricultural right holder, *dian*-holder, lien creditor, lessee, or depositary, or by virtue of some other similar legal relationship, such other person is an indirect possessor."[270] For instance, a landlord who does not have the key to his or her rented house also qualifies as an indirect possessor. An indirect possessor (such as a landlord) and a direct possessor (such as a tenant) are both possessors but not co-possessors.

---

266. For an economic critique of the possession concept adopted in civil-law countries, *see* Yun-chien Chang, *The Economy of Concept and Possession*, *in Law and Economics of Possession* 103 (Yun-chien Chang ed., Cambridge Univ. Press 2015); Yun-chien Chang, *The Problematic Concept of Possession in DCFR: Lessons from Law and Economics of Possession*, 5 Eur. J. Property L. 4 (2016).
267. Norman Barry, *Property Rights in Common and Civil Law*, *in The Elgar Companion to the Economics of Property Rights* 177, 180, 184 (Enrico Colombatto ed., Edward Elgar 2004); Monika Hinteregger, *The Protection of Property Rights*, *in Cases, Materials and Text on Property Law* 97, 98 (Sjef Van Erp & Bram Akkermans eds., Hart 2012).
268. Taiwan Civil Code, Art. 940.
269. Taiwan Civil Code, Art. 942.
270. Taiwan Civil Code, Art. 941.

231. Possession terminates when the original possessor loses actual control. Nevertheless, if the lack of actual control is only temporary, possession does not terminate.[271] Similarly, possession is transferred when the possessed thing is delivered to another person by applying *mutatis mutandis* Article 761, which prescribes how titles to movable properties can be transferred de jure.[272] That is, the original possessor can transfer possession to another person by *traditio,*[273] *attornment,*[274] *constitutum possessorium,*[275] or *traditio brevi manu.*[276]

II. Claims to Restore Possession

232. Like revindication (*see* Chapter 2 of Part I), there are three types of claims to restore possession. If possession of a thing has been deprived, the original possessor can demand its return. If possession is interfered with, the possessor can demand the removal of the interference. If there is a risk of interference, the possessor can demand measures to prevent the risk.[277] The statute of limitation for these claims is one year from the time of the dispossession or interference or from the emergence of the interference risk.[278] A co-possessor can unilaterally claim to restore possession.[279] The returned thing is still co-possessed, rather than possessed solely by the possessor who made the claim.[280]

233. A survey of court cases in 2006–2011 in all levels of courts reveals that courts only infrequently rely on Article 962 to decide cases. No unlawful possessor (such as a thief) has sued another unlawful possessor to restore the former's possession. Possessors who are also property right holders (such as an owner or a holder of *superficies*) do not have to rely on Article 962 either, as they can base their cases on revindication,[281] which is a more effective remedy with less stringent constraints.[282] Those who need Article 962 to win their cases are "*in personam* possessors," namely possessors who acquire their right to possess via contracts, such as

271. Taiwan Civil Code, Art. 964.
272. Taiwan Civil Code, Art. 946.
273. According to *Black's Law Dictionary*, it means: "the simple delivery of a piece of property by one person to another with the intention of transferring ownership."
274. According to *Black's Law Dictionary*, it means: "a constructive delivery involving the transfer of mediate possession while a third person has immediate possession; esp., a bailee's acknowledgment that he or she will hold the chattels on behalf of someone other than the bailor."
275. According to *Black's Law Dictionary*, it means: "a type of constructive delivery in which mediate possession is transferred while the immediate control or custody remains in the transferor."
276. According to *Black's Law Dictionary*, it means: "the surrender of the mediate possession of a thing to the person who is already in immediate possession of it."
277. Taiwan Civil Code, Art. 962.
278. Taiwan Civil Code, Art. 963.
279. Taiwan Civil Code, Art. 963-1.
280. *Ibid.*
281. Taiwan Civil Code, Art. 767.
282. Article 962 can be used when only possession was "deprived" (i.e., forceful dispossession) or "interfered."

leases. These possessors' in personam right to possess is only good against the other contractual party, but not against third parties who deprived them of the original possession.

III. Self-Help

234. Possessors[283] and agents in possession[284] can exert the right of self-help. That is, they can defend themselves with their own force against any act which deprives them of or interferes with their possession. When a real property has been seized, the possessor may expel the tortfeasor immediately after the seizure. In the case of personal property dispossession, possessors and their agents can retrieve it from the tortfeasor on the spot or after pursuit. A co-possessor can unilaterally conduct self-help.[285]

IV. Co-possession

235. Two or more persons who meet the definition of possessions at the same time are co-possessors. Regarding the scope of using possessed things, a co-possessor cannot petition courts to protect his or her possession against other co-possessors.[286] That is, co-possessors have to solve their disputes based on contracts or property rights. If the co-possessors are unlawful possessors without contractual or property relations, courts refuse to intervene as well.

V. Presumptions for Possessors

236. A possessor is presumed to have a legal right that he or she exercises over the possessed thing. This presumption, however, shall not apply when (1) the thing in question is a registered immovable thing; and (2) a person exercises a right other than ownership against the person who gives him or her possession.[287]

237. In addition, possessors are presumed to possess with *animus domini*, in good faith, peacefully, openly, and without fault.[288]

283. Taiwan Civil Code, Art. 960.
284. Taiwan Civil Code, Art. 961.
285. Taiwan Civil Code, Art. 963-1.
286. Taiwan Civil Code, Art. 965.
287. Taiwan Civil Code, Art. 943.
288. Taiwan Civil Code, Art. 944.

VI. Claims and Liabilities of Unlawful Possessors

238. Articles 952–958 of the Taiwan Civil Code delineate the claims and liability of unlawful possessors with regards to a property right holder who demands restoration of possession. Articles 952–955 deal with good-faith unlawful possessors, whereas Articles 956–958 deal with bad-faith unlawful possessors. Possessors are presumed to be good faith (bona fide).[289] A bona fide possessor becomes a mala fide possessor since he is sure that he has no right to possess.[290] Note that it makes the good faith presumption a strong one, as possessors who are "not sure" whether they have the right to possess are still bona fide.

A. Good-Faith Unlawful Possessors

239. Good-faith unlawful possessors can use and profit from the possessed things as long as they are within the scope of their legally presumed right.[291] They can request the person demanding restoration of possession to reimburse "necessary expenses" used to preserve the possessed thing, on the condition that they did not collect legal yields[292] or natural yields of the thing in question.[293] As for "improvement expenses," they should be reimbursed, with a cap of existing added value.[294] Good-faith unlawful possessors have to compensate the person demanding restoration of possession for damages, when the possessed thing is destroyed or damaged, if the former is liable. The compensation is capped at the benefits derived from the destruction and damage.[295]

B. Bad-Faith Unlawful Possessors

240. Bad-faith unlawful possessors have to compensate the person demanding restoration of possession for damages, when the possessed thing is destroyed or damaged, if the former is liable.[296] Bad-faith unlawful possessors cannot demand reimbursement of improvement expenses. As for necessary expenses, the person demanding restoration of possession would need to reimburse the bad-faith unlawful possessors, but the payment shall be capped at the benefits that the former

289. *Ibid.*
290. Taiwan Civil Code, Art. 959.
291. Taiwan Civil Code, Art. 952.
292. Legal yields include, for example, interests and rents. *See* Taiwan Civil Code, Art. 69.
293. Taiwan Civil Code, Art. 954.
294. Taiwan Civil Code, Art. 955.
295. Taiwan Civil Code, Art. 953.
296. Taiwan Civil Code, Art. 956.

received.[297] Bad-faith unlawful possessors have to return the legal yields and natural yields. If the legal yields and natural yields have been consumed, damaged out of negligence, or uncollected, bad-faith unlawful possessors are bound to compensate for their value.[298]

C. *Rarely Used in Practice*

241. Articles 952–958 of the Taiwan Civil Code were rarely used in practice. A survey of cases in all levels of courts in 2008–2012 reveals that courts have relied on these stipulations to make decisions in only four cases.[299]

§2. Acquisitive Prescription (Adverse Possession)

242. Under the adverse possession doctrine, a possessor without legal title, if maintaining actual possession and open, notorious, continuous use of a property for several years, acquires the legal title without compensating the original owner.

243. The acquisitive prescription regime and the relevant administrative rules have been challenged five times in the Constitutional Court of Taiwan. Shih Tzu [Interpretation of Council of Grand Justices[300]] No. 107 essentially concerns acquisitive prescription of public easement. No. 291, No. 350, No. 408, and No. 451 deal with acquisitive prescription of real property rights, and three out of four times the Constitutional Court of Taiwan declared the relevant administrative rules null and void.[301]

I. Ownership of Immovable Things

244. "A person, who has peacefully, publicly and continually possessed another's unregistered real property for twenty years with the intent of being an owner, is entitled to claim to be registered as the owner."[302] "A person, who has peacefully, publicly and continually possessed another's unregistered real property with the intent of being an owner for ten years, and was acting in good faith and not of negligence at the beginning of his possession, is entitled to claim to be registered as the owner."[303]

297. Taiwan Civil Code, Art. 177; Taiwan Civil Code, Art. 957.
298. Taiwan Civil Code, Art. 958.
299. One of us, Yun-chien Chang, conducted this survey.
300. "Council of Grand Justices" is an outdated way of referring to the Constitutional Court of Taiwan. Here we follow the House Style.
301. For the English translation of the Interpretations by the Constitutional Court of Taiwan, visit http://www.judicial.gov.tw/constitutionalcourt/en/p03.asp.
302. Taiwan Civil Code, Art. 769.
303. Taiwan Civil Code, Art. 770.

A. *Presumption*

245. Possessors are presumed to have *animus domini* and the possession is good faith without negligence, peaceful, and conspicuous (public).[304] The presumption saves courts a lot of work in judging the mental state of possessors in matters of adverse possession. It also strongly favors possessors (as compared to original owners), as by default they can draw on the shorter statute of limitation stipulated in Article 770 of the Taiwan Civil Code.

B. *Inherited and Tacked Possession*

246. "The successor or transferee of possession may assert either her own possession or her possession together with that of her predecessor. In cases when the possessor asserts the possession of her predecessor together with that of her own, she succeeds also to its defects."[305]

C. *Change of Possession Intent*

247. A possessor originally without *animus domini* has to notify the person who gave the former actual control about the fact that the former begins to possess the thing in question with *animus domini*. If the person who gave the possessor actual control is not the owner and the possessor knows the identity of the owner, the possessor has to notify the owner as well.[306]

D. *Empirical Survey of Cases*

248. An empirical survey of district court cases in Taiwan between 2006 and 2011 reveals that hardly any possessor successfully gained title through acquisitive prescription. To be exact, only two adverse possessors living in offshore islands prevailed.[307] The main reason is that as of 2012, less than 3.5% of land in Taiwan was unregistered—a prerequisite for acquisitive prescription of real estate ownership. Data from the land registry also reveal that successful acquisitive prescriptions are rare.

---

304. Taiwan Civil Code, Art. 944.
305. Taiwan Civil Code, Art. 947.
306. Taiwan Civil Code, Art. 945.
307. Yun-chien Chang, *Venerable or Outdated? A Radical Proposal to Reform Prescriptive Acquisition Law in Taiwan*, 18 Academia Sinica L. J. 195 (2016).

II. Limited Property Rights of Immovable Things

249. The aforementioned acquisitive prescription doctrine applies *mutatis mutandis* to the acquisition of limited property rights, even when the movable things were registered.[308]

250. An empirical survey of district court cases in Taiwan between 2006 and 2011 reveals that four possessors successfully gained limited property rights through acquisitive prescription. In three of the four cases, the possessor acquired *superficies*. A major reason for the low success rate is that courts have misconstrued the doctrine and added excessive and unreasonable requirements to adverse possessors. Namely, a majority of courts require that, first, as Article 944 of the Taiwan Civil Code presumes possessors to have *animus domini* (which does NOT include the intent to become holders of limited property rights), possessors have to prove this intent with subjective evidence. That is, proof of using the land as a, say, holder of *superficies* is not sufficient. Possessors must show that they know the differences among *superficies*, agricultural rights, *dian*, and easement and that they hold a specific intent to acquire a specific limited property right throughout the statutory period. Understandably, few can meet this burden of proof.[309]

III. Ownership of Movable Things

251. "A person, who has peacefully, publicly and continually possessed another's personal property with the intent of being an owner for ten years, acquires the ownership of such personal property."[310] "A person, who has peacefully, publicly and continually possessed another's personal property with the intent of being an owner for five years, and was in good faith and not of negligence at the beginning of his possession, acquires the ownership of such personal property" (Taiwan Civil Code 768-1).[311]

252. A survey of court cases between 2006 and 2011 reveals that only eleven district court cases involve acquisitive prescription of movable things.[312] In only one case, the possessor (of stones and rocks) successfully acquired ownership through prescription.

308. Taiwan Civil Code, Art. 772.
309. For a critique of this subjective approach in more details, *see ibid.*
310. Taiwan Civil Code, Art. 768.
311. Taiwan Civil Code, Art. 768-1.
312. Yun-chien Chang, *Acquisitive Prescription of Chattels*, 255 Taiwan L. R. 133–140 (2016).

§3. First Possession

253. Whoever possesses unowned movable things with *animus domini* acquires ownership.[313] While the Taiwan Civil Code contains the venerable first possession doctrine, courts seldom find a case to apply it. Between 2006 and 2011, a survey of court cases reveals that no court has relied on the first possession doctrine to adjudicate a dispute regarding movable things.[314] Nonetheless, a case has analogized the first possession doctrine to buildings![315] (Pursuant to Article 10 of the Land Act, unowned land is state-owned.)

§4. Finders as Keepers

254. This section discusses entitlement to lost chattels. In addition to what ordinary people would classify as lost chattels, those discussed here also include floating things, sunken things, and other things that are separated from their possessors due to natural forces.[316] The idiom "finders keepers, losers weepers" does not reflect the law of Taiwan, as the complicated stipulations below show.

I. Duty to Report

255. The finder of a lost thing has a duty to notify its owner[317] as soon as possible or report to the police or local governments and deposit the thing with them at the time of report. However, a person finding a lost thing at public spaces can also report to the manager of such spaces and deposit the thing. Those receiving the report shall announce, broadcast, or use other appropriate means to make the lost and found information known as soon as possible at the place where the thing has been found or at other suitable places.[318]

256. In practice, government agencies create web pages, even websites, to make lost and found information publicly available. Companies operating public transportation such as the Taiwan High Speed Rail or Taipei Metro have lost and found counters in major stations.

257. If owners do not claim lost things within a reasonable time after the aforementioned notice, managers of these public spaces should deposit the lost things

---

313. Taiwan Civil Code, Art. 802.
314. Yun-chien Chang, *First Possession*, 251 Taiwan L. R. 226 (2016).
315. Tai Wan Tai Nan Di Fang Fa Yuan 91 Nian Du Su Zi Di 1944 Hao Min Shi Pan Jue [District Court 2002 No. 1994 Decision].
316. Taiwan Civil Code, Art. 810.
317. Article 803 of the Taiwanese Civil Code lists three types of persons as entitled to receive notifications: an owner, the one who lost the property, and an entitled receiver. In this section, I use "owner" for short.
318. Taiwan Civil Code, Art. 803.

with the police or local governments, which can give notice again shall they consider the original notices inappropriate.[319]

II. Reward

258. If lost chattels are claimed within six months from the date of the last notice, the aforementioned finders, managers, the police, or local governments shall return the lost chattels after owners have reimbursed those who have incurred expenses for notice and preservation.[320]

259. Finders are entitled to claim from owners a reward that shall not exceed 10% of the property value. When lost chattels do not have monetary value, finders are still entitled to claim a moderate reward. If paying the aforementioned rewards would be utterly unfair, owners can petition courts to reduce or waive their obligation to give rewards. Claims for rewards will be extinguished by prescription, if they are not exercised within six months. A person or an institute which incurs notice or preservation expenses or a finder entitled to a reward has a retention right over the lost movable thing until such expenses or rewards have been paid. If several persons have claims for reimbursements or rewards, possessors of lost chattels are presumed to possess for them all.[321]

260. "Finders have no claim for rewards in one of the following situations: (1) A lost thing was found in public spaces or common carriers by managers or employees working there. (2) Finders failed to notify or deposit within seven days or concealed their finding upon inquiry. (3) Owners or receivers from lower-income households accepted emergency or disaster relief."[322]

261. These stipulations might be the only Book of Things content that has attracted public attention and, indeed, public outrage. When enacted in 1930, the reward was a fixed "30% of property value." The rigidity and practical difficulty led to the 2009 amendment that changed the reward to "up to 30% of property value." In 2012, a college student who majored in law found chattels of a poor person and demanded the maximum 30% reward. The finder immediately became the enemy of the public in this media age. The legislature responded and amended the reward to "up to 10%." Article 805-1 of the Taiwan Civil Code was also added to ensure that poor people who lose a fortune would not have to pay an unbearable reward to get back their chattels.

319. Taiwan Civil Code, Art. 804.
320. Taiwan Civil Code, Art. 805.
321. Taiwan Civil Code, Art. 805.
322. Taiwan Civil Code, Art. 805-1.

III. Auction

262. If a lost thing is corrupt-prone, or its preservation expenses are excessive, it can be sold by auction or at market price. The proceeds shall be kept on behalf of the original owners.[323]

IV. Prescription Period: Six Months

263. "If lost chattels are not claimed within six months from the date of the last notice, finders become owners of the chattels. The police or local governments should notify finders to pick up the chattels or proceeds. If personal notification is not feasible, the police or local governments should give a public notice."[324]

264. "If finders do not claim such chattels or proceeds within three months from the date of notice, the lost chattels or proceeds belong to the cities or counties where the lost chattels or proceeds have been kept."[325]

V. Fast-Track

265. When the value of lost chattels is less than New Taiwan Dollars (TWD) 500 (about USD 17 in 2015), the aforementioned procedure has to be followed, but finders can become owners in fifteen days.[326]

VI. Treasure Trove

266. "Whoever finds a treasure trove and takes possession of it acquires its ownership. However, if the treasure trove is found in a personal or real property owned by another, the finder and the owner of such a personal or real property shall each acquire a half of the treasure trove."[327] Nonetheless, when a treasure trove has great academic, artistic, archaeological, or historical value, its ownership shall be determined by other statutes such as the Cultural Heritage Preservation Act and the Act for State-owned Assets.[328]

323. Taiwan Civil Code, Art. 806.
324. Taiwan Civil Code, Art. 807.
325. Taiwan Civil Code, Art. 807.
326. Taiwan Civil Code, Art. 807-1.
327. Taiwan Civil Code, Art. 808.
328. Taiwan Civil Code, Art. 809.

§5. Bona Fide Purchaser

267. The basic bona fide purchase rule is that "when a transferee of a personal property is in possession of it and is protected by the provisions concerning possession, he acquires ownership of the thing even if the transferor has no right to transfer such ownership."[329] The critical condition in this stipulation is "protection by possession provisions," which is elaborated in Articles 948–951-1 of the Taiwan Civil Code. Note that Article 886 of the Taiwan Civil Code contains a similar stipulation on bona fide acquisition of pledge, which also links to the provisions in Articles 948–951-1 of the Taiwan Civil Code.[330]

268. A survey of cases in all levels of courts in Taiwan in 2006–2012 reveals that the bona fide purchase doctrine was drawn on by courts in only fifty-two cases.[331] The chattels that have become the things in disputes include cars, logs, gravel, electric lines, street lamps, machines, etc.

I. Voluntarily Dispossessed Chattels

269. When a transferor has no right to transfer ownership or limited property rights of a movable thing, but a transferee is bona fide, the latter's possession is still protected by law—this clause, when viewed together with Article 801 of the Taiwan Civil Code, means that a transferee acquires the property right nonetheless.[332] If a transferee's good faith is because of his or her gross negligence, he or she will not enjoy the protection of possession law.[333] A transferee has to be bona fide at the time of the actual delivery (*traditio*), if *constitutum possessorium* was used as the method to transfer possession.[334]

II. Involuntarily Dispossessed Chattels

270. If the thing in question was stolen, lost or, otherwise dispossessed involuntarily, a bona fide transferee does not immediately acquire titles upon delivery. Rather, an original possessor has two years since dispossession to demand the bona fide, current possessor to return the possessed chattels. Once returned, an original possessor's rights on the movable thing are retroactively restored.[335]

---

329. Taiwan Civil Code, Art. 801.
330. Only three cases in 2006–2012 involve *bona fide* transferee of pledge. Yun-chien Chang. *An Economic Analysis of Good-faith Purchase of Chattels*, 21 Academia Sinica Law Journal 81 (2017).
331. *See ibid.*
332. Taiwan Civil Code, Art. 948.
333. *Ibid.*
334. *Ibid.* In only one case in 2006–2012, *constitutum possessorium* was used as the method to transfer possession.
335. Taiwan Civil Code, Art. 949.

A. Market Overt Rule

271. If a bona fide transferee buys an involuntarily dispossessed thing in an open market or from a merchant dealer, the original possessor has to reimburse the bona fide transferee for the paid price in order to restore possession of the movable thing in question.[336] No court decisions appear to have defined the market overt rule in a more specific way. One case has ruled that the stock market is an open market,[337] whereas two cases have rendered that pawn shops are neither open market nor merchant dealer/sellers, so Article 950 of the Taiwan Civil Code is not applicable.[338]

B. Exception

272. If money or bearer instruments are involuntarily dispossessed, the original possessor cannot demand a bona fide transferee to return possession.[339]

III. Bad-Faith Original Possessor

273. Note that Articles 948–951 of the Taiwan Civil Code balance the interests between a good-faith "possessor" and an original "possessor" (rather than an original owner). Article 951-1 of the Taiwan Civil Code makes this more explicit by excluding protection for original possessors if they are *mala fide* and unlawful. In other words, lawful possessors and bona fide unlawful possessors are protected.

---

336. Taiwan Civil Code, Art. 950.
337. Tai Wan Gao Deng Fa Yuan Tai Zhong Fen Yuan 96 Nian Du Zhong Zai Geng (1) Zi Di 1 Hao Min Shi Pan Jue [High Court 2007 No. 1 Decision].
338. Tai Wan Tai Bei Di Fang Fa Yuan 96 Nian Du Jian Shang Zi Di 111 Hao Min Shi Pan Jue [District Court 2007 No. 111 Decision]; Tai Wan Tai Bei Di Fang Fa Yuan 95 Nian Du Bei Jian Zi Di 57353 Hao Min Shi Jian Yi Pan Jue [District Court 2006 No. 57353 Decision].
339. Taiwan Civil Code, Art. 951.

Chapter 4. Accession

274. The accession principle covers *specificatio, accessio, confusio,* and some other related doctrines.[340] *Specificatio* arises when a person's labor is mixed with another's thing, whereas *accessio* and *confusio* arise when two things owned by different parties are combined or intermingled, respectively.

§1. *Accessio* and *Confusio*

I. *Accessio* of a Movable Thing and an Immovable Thing

275. If a movable thing is combined with an immovable thing (building or land)[341] in such a way that the former becomes an "essential part" of the latter, the ownership of the immovable thing extends to the movable thing.[342]

II. *Accessio* of Multiple Movable Things

276. If two movable things are combined in such a way that they cannot be separated without being damaged or incurring excessive expenses, the previous owners become co-owners of this thing. Nonetheless, when one of the things can be regarded as the "principal thing," its owner acquires the sole ownership but has to compensate the other owner.[343] The opposite of a principal thing is an "accessory thing." An accessory thing is not part of a principal thing, but the former usually facilitates the utilization of the latter,[344] like a TV set and its remote control. The disposition of a principal thing extends to its accessories. In the Taiwan Civil Code, a principal thing and an accessory thing have to belong to the same owner.

III. *Confusio*

277. When two or more things are intermingled and no longer distinguishable from each other (or cannot be distinguished without incurring excessive expenses), the previous owners become co-owners of the thing(s). Nonetheless, when one of the things can be regarded as the "principal thing," its owner acquires the sole ownership but has to compensate the other owner.[345]

---

340. *See* Thomas W. Merrill, *Accession and Original Ownership*, 1 J. Legal Analysis 459, 464 (2009).
341. For an economic analysis of *accessio* and *confusio*, *see* Yun-chien Chang, *Property Law with Chinese Characteristics: An Economic and Comparative Analysis*, 1 Brigham-Kanner Property Rights Conf. J. 345 (2012).
342. Taiwan Civil Code, Art. 811.
343. Taiwan Civil Code, Arts. 812, 816.
344. Taiwan Civil Code, Art. 68.
345. Taiwan Civil Code, Art. 813.

§2. *Specificatio*

278. Under this doctrine, if the value of the improved thing relative to that of the unimproved thing is high enough, the improver will gain title but will have to compensate the owner for the value of the object before the improvements were undertaken. If the improver fails to significantly increase the value of the property, the original owner can keep the property, but the owner has to compensate the improver for his or her labor and other inputs. Whether the improver of personal property knows about his or her lack of property rights or not, the knowledge does not affect the application of the *specificatio*[346] doctrine.[347]

§3. The Aftermath

279. When the ownership of a personal property is extinguished pursuant to the accession principle, all other rights over such personal property are also extinguished.[348]

280. The person who suffers from a loss pursuant to the accession principle—such as an owner of accessory things in *accessio* and *confusio* and an owner who loses title because improvers greatly increase the value of the thing in question—is entitled to reimbursement of the value.[349]

§4. Fructus Naturales Doctrine

281. Unless otherwise stipulated, parts and natural yields of things, when separated, still belong to owners of the things.[350] Persons with profit rights acquire titles to the natural yields.[351] Natural yields include, for instance, fruits and new-born animals.[352]

§5. Accretion

282. A riparian landowner whose land is gradually augmented by alluvial formations has priority to acquire the ownership of newly formed land according to law.[353]

346. For an economic analysis of specificatio, *see* Yun-chien Chang, *An Economic and Comparative Analysis of Specificatio (the Accession Doctrine)*, 39 Eur. J. L. & Econ. 225 (2014).
347. Taiwan Civil Code, Arts. 814, 816.
348. Taiwan Civil Code, Art. 815.
349. Taiwan Civil Code, Art. 816.
350. Taiwan Civil Code, Art. 766.
351. Taiwan Civil Code, Art. 70.
352. Taiwan Civil Code, Art. 69.
353. Land Act, Art. 13.

Chapter 5. Appropriation

283. Appropriation is not a property concept in Taiwan. Thus, it is not covered in this monograph. To the extent that appropriation relates to trespass and the protection of ownership, *see* the discussion of revindication in Chapter 2 of Part I.

Chapter 6. Expropriation*

§1. Background: Stipulations Outside the Civil Code

284. The Taiwan Civil Code does not contain any stipulation regarding expropriation (or, condemnation). The law governing expropriation is mainly the Land Expropriation Act. Before introducing the relevant statutes, a brief tour of the constitutional foundation is warranted.

285. The Constitution of Taiwan fails to include a "just compensation" clause or a "public use" clause. Article 143, Section 1 of the Constitution of Taiwan *does* prescribe that "[a]ll land within the territory of the Republic of China shall belong to the whole body of citizens. Private ownership of land, acquired by the people in accordance with law, shall be protected and restricted by law. Privately-owned land shall be liable to taxation according to its value, and the Government may buy such land according to its value." As the final clause (buy … land) is not interpreted to mean expropriation, the constitution provides little guidance in determining the scope and limit of eminent domain. However, the Constitutional Court is not entirely absent from this scene. In fact, in a number of constitutional interpretations,[354] the Constitutional Court constructed the constitutional mandates regarding the governmental use of the eminent domain power. These mandates constitute the outline of expropriation law in Taiwan.

286. Since 2000, the Land Expropriation Act has been the major source of law for takings of land and buildings. Before then, expropriation stipulations were scattered in many different statutes. Now, pursuant to Article 1 of the Land Expropriation Act, "Land expropriation shall be governed by this Act. Matters not provided in this Act shall be governed by other applicable laws. Where other laws are inconsistent with this Act with regard to expropriation procedures and expropriation compensation standards, this Act shall prevail." Hence, this chapter frequently turns to the Land Expropriation Act and the regulations stipulated to complement the Land Expropriation Act.

§2. Public Interest

287. Public interest and necessity are the two key criteria to meet before the state exercises its eminent domain power. Article 15 of the Taiwanese Constitution protects private property rights, and Article 23 includes a long list of constitutional interpretations that have established that private property rights and other human

* This chapter is adapted from Yun-chien Chang, *Eminent Domain Law in Taiwan: New Law, Old Practice?, in Eminent Domain: A Comparative Perspective* 93–117 (Iljoong Kim, Hojun Lee & Ilya Somin eds., 2017).

354. Judicial Yuan Interpretation Nos. 110, 215, 236, 336, 400, 409, 425, 440, 508, 513, 516, 534, 579, and 652.

rights can be limited, if commensurate with the "proportionality principle."[355] Article 3 of the Land Expropriation Act further spells out that takings must be "for public interest purposes" and "to the extent strictly required." These two criteria are abstract. Unfortunately, neither the Constitutional Court nor the Supreme Administrative Court has developed clearer tests to implement these two statutory requirements. Administrative courts, in particular, have been extremely deferential to the government in these two matters, essentially giving the latter a blank check.

288. Takings of real properties are further limited to certain undertakings. Article 3 of the Land Expropriation Act first lists nine concrete undertakings:

(1) national defense;
(2) communication or transportation;
(3) public utility enterprises;
(4) water conservancy;
(5) public health and environmental protection;
(6) government office buildings, office buildings of local self-governing bodies, and other public buildings;
(7) educational, academic and cultural undertakings;
(8) social welfare;
(9) state-owned enterprises.

289. Then Article 3 of the Land Expropriation Act is willing to accommodate "other undertakings for which land may be expropriated according to law." The devil is in the details. The Ministry of the Interior, the central competent agency in charge of the Land Expropriation Act, has identified about thirty other statutes that authorize expropriation of real estates. Due to the open-ended nature of the list, the legislature can at any time expand the scope of takings without amending the high-profile Land Expropriation Act.

290. In response to the several controversies in 2011 regarding condemnation of premium farmland to build science parks, Article 3-1 of the Land Expropriation Act, added in 2011, stipulates that for agricultural land, "the competent authority in charge of the relevant industry should give consideration to the public interest purpose and necessity of expropriation at the time of designation or rezoning … .If the agricultural land located within the land selected by a land use applicant is exempted from the approval of the regional plan preparing authority with regard to its rezoning, the approval of the agriculture authority under the municipal or county (city) government shall first be obtained before the land is changed to non-agricultural use." Premium agricultural land, according to the last paragraph of

355. For application of the proportionality principle in Taiwan and other East Asian countries, *see* Chengyi Huang & David Law, *Proportionality Review of Administrative Action in Japan, Korea, Taiwan, and China, in Research Handbook in Comparative Law and Regulation* (Francesca Bignami & David Zaring eds., Edward Elgar 2015).

Article 3-1 of the Land Expropriation Act, in principle cannot be condemned, unless odd pieces of such land are interspersed and it is difficult to circumvent condemning it.[356]

291. Moreover, the also newly enacted Article 3-2 of the Land Expropriation Act requires a comprehensive assessment of the public interest and necessity of the takings project. The legislature even lays out the variables to be considered:

1. Social factors: Including the size of population affected by the expropriation, the age structure of the affected population, and the extent of effects of the expropriation plan on the current status of the surrounding communities, the lifestyle of and health risk to disadvantaged groups.
2. Economic factors: Including the effects of the expropriation plan on tax revenue, food security, increase/decrease in jobs or population that might be forced to change jobs, the costs of expropriation, public facilities required of governments at all levels, the fiscal expenditure and burden of governments, the agriculture, forestry, fishery, or animal husbandry industry chain and the integrity of land use.
3. Cultural and ecological factors: Including changes in natural urban/rural sceneries, cultural relics, living conditions or life style caused by the expropriation plan, and its impacts on the ecological environment of the area, surrounding residents or the society as a whole.
4. Sustainable development factors: Including national sustainable development policies, sustainability indicators, and national land use planning.
5. Others: Other relevant factors or factors that should be evaluated based on the individual expropriation plan.

292. The Ministry of the Interior reviews the assessment of public interest and necessity. Articles 2, 14, and 15 of the Land Expropriation Act prescribe that the Ministry of the Interior establish a "Takings Review Task Force."[357] Articles 13 and 13-1 authorize the Ministry of the Interior, through the Takings Review Task Force, to review the assessment of public interest and necessity, among others. The Ministry of the Interior, in two administrative rules announced in 2011 and 2012, requires an additional review of public interest and necessity for certain takings projects[358] in an earlier stage of the whole process. The two-time reviews have to be substantive and de novo each time.

---

356. Article 3-1 of the Land Expropriation Act also details that the exceptions to this no-taking principle are takings for "national defense, communication or transportation, or water conservancy undertaking; a public utility enterprise for erecting power transmission lines; or for use in an infrastructure project already approved by the Executive Yuan."
357. The Task Force consists of seventeen members. Eight members are officials from several relevant government agencies. Nine members are scholars, experts, and representatives of private organizations.
358. More specifically, these takings projects (1) are implemented as zone expropriation; (2) involve certain undertakings (e.g., building or establishing export zones, science parks, produce markets, airports); (3) expand urban planning; or (4) develop more than 30 hectares.

§3. Who Can Exercise the Eminent Domain Power?

293. Only the state can exercise eminent domain power. The Ministry of the Interior has the power to approve or disapprove a takings project as the designated organ of the state.[359] The more important question under Taiwanese law is who can apply as a "land use applicant" to the Ministry of the Interior for condemning real properties. In theory, private (legal) persons can be land use applicants, but in practice, no statute has authorized any private parties to become land use applicants. According to Article 15 of the Enforcement Rules for the Land Expropriation Act, central government agencies, city governments, county governments, town governments, and irrigation associations[360] are land use applicants.

§4. Just Compensation

294. One of us has elsewhere provided theoretical analysis and empirical examinations of takings compensation law in Taiwan in 1954–1977[361] and 1977–2012.[362] The laws summarized here are the latest, post-2012 revisions of the Land Expropriation Act, which revolutionarily reforms the compensation law. Before the reform, land value was assessed by combining a pre-determined and under-assessed official land value with a pre-determined extra bonus. After the reform, market value of land should be used to compensate condemnees. While land value is a major component of the compensation package, it is not the only one. Section I describes all the elements of takings compensation. Section II then focuses on how market value of land has been appraised since 2012.

I. The Elements of Takings Compensation

295. Total takings compensation includes that for land; constructional improvements (such as a house); agricultural improvements (such as trees); incurred expenses for land improvements; business losses and relocation expenses. Takings compensation "shall be paid within fifteen days after the expiration of the public announcement period,"[363] and the public announcement period is thirty days after the city/county government, upon receiving the notice of approval from the Ministry of the Interior, makes a public announcement and notifies condemnees.[364] Except for land value compensation (which is discussed in Section B), the appraisal methods for these compensations will be introduced in turn.[365]

359. Land Expropriation Act, Art. 14.
360. Irrigation associations are *public* legal persons in Taiwan law.
361. Yun-chien Chang, "Empire Building and Fiscal Illusion? An Empirical Study of Government Official Behaviors in Takings." *Journal of Empirical Legal Studies* 6 (3) (2009): 541–584.
362. Yun-chien Chang, Empire Building and Fiscal Illusion? An Empirical Study of Government Official Behaviors in Takings, 6 J. Empirical Legal Stud. 541 (2009).
363. Land Expropriation Act, Art. 20.
364. Land Expropriation Act, Art. 18.
365. I omit the discussion of compensation for contiguous land (not condemned but affected).

296. Compensation for constructional improvements equals "replacement cost at the time of expropriation."[366] The city/county governments (the first-level local governments in Taiwan) are responsible for calculating the replacement costs themselves or commissioning real estate appraisers to do the work. Only legal buildings are eligible for compensation.[367]

297. Compensation for agricultural improvements "shall be determined based on the value of the ripened crops thereof, provided the crops are due to ripen in less than one year from the date of expropriation, or based on the cost incurred in their planting and cultivation with reference to their current value, provided the crops are due to ripen in more than one year from the date of expropriation."[368] The Ministry of the Interior has enacted incredibly detailed tables for determining the compensable value of various types of trees and flowers.

298. According to the relevant laws and regulations, landowners who have incurred expenses for improving land (such as constructing a conduit or a dam and paving a road) and who have stopped renovating upon learning of the forthcoming expropriation can receive reimbursement for the expenses.[369]

299. Article 33 of the Land Expropriation Act stipulates that "[i]f the expropriated land or land improvement was originally provided for legal business operations, the loss sustained due to the cessation of business or shrinkage of business scale as a result of land or land improvement expropriation shall be compensated." Note that, again, only legal businesses will be compensated. The Ministry of the Interior designed a formula to compute positive business losses. Firms that are losing money will, of course, not receive compensation.

300. Relocation expenses are a combination of different fees related to moving. In short, the following items are compensable: moving fees for graves, memorials, and constructions that owners prefer relocating; moving fees for residents whose household registration records show that they are in residence six months before the takings notice is posted; moving fees for large machinery, livestock, etc. There are assessment standards for each category.

II. Appraisal of Land Value

301. Assessment of land value is the most complicated and controversial part of determining the amount of takings compensation, as appraisal of land value now is *not* formulaic and land value takes up a lion's share of the total takings compensation. Before 2012, determining the compensable land value was mechanical. One

366. Land Expropriation Act, Art. 31.
367. For a study on illegal buildings in Taiwan, *see* Yun-chien Chang & Henry E. Smith, *The Numerus Clausus Principle, Property Custom, and the Emergence of New Property Forms*, 100 Iowa L. Rev. 2275 (2015).
368. Land Expropriation Act, Art. 31.
369. Land Expropriation Act, Art. 32.

of us has shown that a majority of condemnees were under-compensated under the old regime, which relied on official land value for tax purposes in the critical calculation.[370] This section introduces and evaluates the new regime.

302. Condemnees shall receive "current market value" as compensation for expropriation of their land.[371] The Land Value Evaluation Committee in each city/county government determines the current market value.[372] The Committee is not itself an agency; rather, it makes decisions in the name of the local city/county government. The compensation is paid from the budget of the land use applicant. Below is a summary of how current market value is assessed and adjusted.

303. The current market value is appraised by either local governments themselves or real estate appraisers commissioned by local governments. Both have to follow the Regulations on Appraising Current Market Value for Takings Compensation Purposes in assessing the value of condemned land. In short, the Regulation prescribes that the comparable sale approach (also known as the market data approach) is the principle, and the income capitalization approach is the exception.

304. More specifically, in principle, appraising current market value for takings compensation purposes can be broken down into several steps:[373]

(1) collecting or revising all kinds of maps (such as urban planning and zoning maps);
(2) collecting information on real estate sales between March 2 and September 1 of the "baseline year" (Y_1);
(3) demarcating the jurisdictions into "land value zones" by land value, zoning, infrastructure, among others;
(4) estimating the "normal"[374] adjusted-to-September-1st unit price (Taiwan Dollars per square meter) of the collected sales;
(5) among the collected sale, choosing three comparable land parcels within the land value zones where the takings project in question takes place;
   (a) comparing with the comparable land parcels and estimating the unit price of the condemned land;
   (b) submitting the estimations to Land Value Evaluation Committee for approval or adjustment. The approved unit land will then be used for condemnations taking place in the next, "current year" (Y_2=Y_1+1).[375]

370. Yun-chien Chang, *Private Property and Takings Compensation: Theoretical Framework and Empirical Analysis* (Edward Elgar 2013).
371. Land Expropriation Act Art. 30.
372. This committee has 17–19 members, and comprises the (deputy) mayor, a local legislator, five local government officials, and several representatives from relevant associations.
373. Regulations on Appraising Current Market Value for Takings Compensation, Arts. 4–21.
374. The Regulations on Appraising Current Market Value for Takings Compensation Purposes specifies rules for appraisers to adjust the abnormality of the sale prices.
375. There are exceptions; details are omitted here.

305. Market value of land fluctuates on a daily basis, so an up-to-date land value has to be estimated for land expropriations that take place after July 1 of the current year. An adjustment ratio should be computed based on the relative estimated price on September 1 of the baseline year and March 1 of the current year.[376] Since August 2012, the actual sale prices of all real estate transactions have to be reported to the government. Thus, the government now has a firm grasp of the market value of land. Since 2014, the actual sale price data were used to compute the adjustment ratio. More specifically, local governments compare the average sale prices of comparable properties whose unit prices are between the 25th percentile and the 75th percentile in both the baseline period (March 2 to September 1 of the baseline year) and the current period (September 2 of the baseline year to March 1 of the current year) to estimate the percentage changes in land value.[377]That is, the 25% highest and 25% lowest unit prices are excluded. The average prices of the rest of the unit prices in both periods are calculated separately and then compared. Adjustment ratio=average price in the current period / average price in the baseline period. Finally, the estimations of adjustment ratios should be sent to Land Value Evaluation Committee for approval or adjustment.

306. In principle, condemnees receive the up-to-date current market value as compensation. Takings projects finalized between January 1 and June 30 of the current year should use the current market value estimated on the basis of market value on September 1 of the baseline year. Those closed in the second half of the current year should use the aforementioned market value adjusted by the adjustment ratio, to update the current market value to March 1 of the current year. An exception: if the current market value of the baseline year has been publicly announced and notified to the condemnees, and the adjusted current market value of the current year is lower than the former value, the higher market value of the baseline year shall still be used to compensate the condemnees.[378]

§5. The Negotiated Purchase Procedure

307. In principle, land use applicants have to negotiate in good faith and in their best efforts with the owners of the land needed for the undertakings, before applying to the Ministry of the Interior for expropriation.[379] Land use applicants should bargain with the owners based on "market value."[380] In both the negotiated purchase here and the takings setting, the legislature uses market value as the standard

376. March 1 of the current year is six months after September 1 of the baseline year. September 1, as described in the text, is the baseline date for adjusting sale prices of comparable land. Art. 30 of the Land Expropriation Act prescribes that local governments have to investigate market conditions every six months.
377. Tu Di Zheng Shou Bu Chang Shi Jia Cha Gu Ban Fa [Regulations on Appraising Current Market Value for Market Value for Takings Compensation Purposes], Arts. 26, 29.
378. Tu Di Zheng Shou Tiao Li Shi Xing Xi Ze [Enforcement Rules for the Land Expropriation Act], Art. 30.
379. Land Expropriation Act, Art. 11.
380. Land Expropriation Act, Art. 11.

for compensation. Nonetheless, Article 30 of the Land Expropriation Act stipulates that the market value in the takings procedure has to be approved by the Land Value Evaluation Committee, while Article 11 of the Land Expropriation Act defines market value as a "mean normal transaction price in the market" without designating any agency or committee to approve the estimated market value. The Ministry of the Interior has advised land use applicants that the market value used in the negotiated purchase procedure need not equate the market value approved by the Land Value Evaluation Committee; in fact, a hard, non-negotiable bottom-line is the antithesis of the spirit of negotiated purchase.

Chapter 7. Insolvency

308. Insolvency, or personal bankruptcy, is not considered a property law issue in Taiwan and falls outside of the expertise of the co-authors. The Bankruptcy Act (revised as of 1993) and the Consumer Insolvency Act (revised as of 2012) are the special statutes that govern insolvency problems in Taiwan.

Part IV. Trust

Chapter 1. Introduction

309. The Trust Act[381] of Taiwan (hereafter, TTA) was promulgated in 1995 and came into force in 1996.[382] The Act was heavily influenced by the Japanese Trust Act promulgated in 1922 which primarily adopted common-law principles with some modifications. Therefore, it can be said that common-law trusts law was imported into Taiwan via Japan. Being a versatile legal regime, trusts can be used for various purposes (i.e., investment, estate-planning, charity, securitization, etc.). However, it cannot be denied that most trusts are created for commercial purposes (i.e., unit-trust, asset-backed securitization, or land-developing schemes). This shows that trust law in Taiwan is traditionally regarded as a finance-oriented legal institution, though it is not necessarily one. Whatever the case may be, the Trust Act functions as infrastructure for all types of trust relationship created. The following sections elucidate the contents and main features of the Act.

Figure 6 shows that trust has been steadily used and used more often many limited property forms.

381. The official translation uses the term "trust law" (*see* http://law.moj.gov.tw). However, the term does not correctly tell us that this is a statute. Thus, this work adopts the term "Trust Act."

382. The term "trust" first appeared in the Banking Act promulgated in 1931 in order to meet commercial demand to establish trust investment companies. However, no detailed rules of trust law were provided for in this act. For more details about the brief history of trust law in Taiwan, *see* Wang Wen-Yeu, Wang Chieh-Cheng & Shieh Jer-Sheng, *Trust Law in Taiwan: History, Current Features and Future Prospects, in Trust Law in Asian Civil Law Jurisdictions: A Comparative Analysis* 63 (Lusina Ho & Rebecca Lee eds., Oxford Univ. Press 2013).

Figure 6 Number of Registration Filing, Trust, 2006–2019

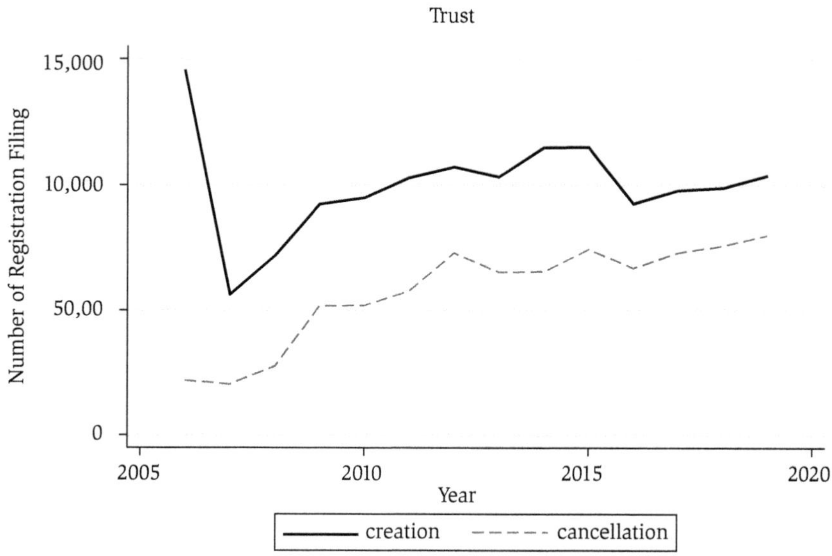

Data source: The Ministry of the Interior, Taiwan.
Graph created by the authors.

Chapter 2. Creation of the Trust

§1. Three Ways in Which a Trust Can Come About

310. The term "trust" in the Trust Act denotes a legal relationship in which property (either personal or real) is vested in a trustee who is obliged to administer or dispose of the property for the benefit of a beneficiary or for a specified purpose.[383] There are three ways in which a trust can arise. A person (i.e., the settlor) can create a trust by concluding a *trust contract* with the trustee (i.e., an *inter vivos* trust), or by making a *will* (i.e., a testamentary trust).[384] It is also possible for a settlor to set up a trust by *declaring himself trustee* of the trust (i.e., the self-declaration of trust). The self-declaration of trust is, however, restricted to charitable trusts, and the settlor must be a legal entity. Furthermore, the settlor must obtain the government's permission before making a self-declaration of charitable trust.[385] These limitations are designed mainly to prevent self-declarations of trust from being used by people intending to damage their personal creditors. One further issue needs exploring in regard to the concept of trust *contract*. The key issue here is whether it is plausible to regard trust as a type of contract. The present authors argue it is not, for there would be, *inter alia*, a contradiction germane to the underlying nature of trustees' liability between a trust created by a contract and that by a will. Obviously, we cannot imagine a trustee under a testamentary trust owes any contractual liability in breach of trust, while it is fully possible to think that a trustee under a trust contract owes contractual liability should he breach the trust. However, the story goes awry when we find the identical breach results in liability of a different nature, which can scarcely be accepted. It must be noted that trusts are not contracts in common-law jurisdictions, and, moreover, the trust provided for in Book X of the DCFR does not adopt a contractual approach either, to which Taiwanese legislature may need to pay careful attention.

§2. Void and Voidable Trusts

311. Trusts are *void*:[386] (1) if their purpose involves violating statutes containing mandatory rules; (2) if their purpose is contrary to public policy; (3) if they are established solely for the purpose of litigation since a case should be delegated to a qualified lawyer if it is to be delegated at all; or (4) if the trustee holds a right for a beneficiary who is prohibited by law from holding that right. This may happen in a situation where foreigners are not allowed to own land, yet a trust of it is created for the benefit of a foreigner: the trust, in this case, is void, for it evades the prohibitive rules by transforming the right into a beneficial interest. The most common ground for a trust to be *voidable* is found in the case where a debtor/settlor creates a trust in order to prejudice his or her own creditors since the fund would be immune

383. Trust Act, Art. 1.
384. Trust Act, Art. 2.
385. Trust Act, Art. 71.
386. Trust Act, Art. 5.

to the debtor/settlor's bankruptcy. It is carved out of the debtor's personal patrimony so as to avoid execution carried out by his or her creditors. The trust so created can be set aside (i.e., made voidable) by the debtor's creditors.[387]

387. Trust Act, Art. 6(1).

Chapter 3. Trust Fund

§1. A Segregated Fund

312. The trust fund refers to the rights (either personal or proprietary) held by a trustee under a trust.[388] Those rights substituting for the initial rights also comprise a trust fund[389] under the doctrine of real subrogation. Once a trust fund is operating, the law produces a series of effects to safeguard the fund. First, the fund does not appertain to the trustee's estate upon his death.[390] Second, the fund does not fall within the scope of the trustee's personal estate should he become bankrupt (i.e., the so-called bankruptcy effect).[391] Third, neither the personal creditors of the settlor, nor those of the trustee, can recoup their loss from the trust fund.[392] However, there are two exceptions to this effect: when those rights of the settlor's personal creditors were created before the creation of the trust, or when those rights of the trustee's personal creditors arise from the management of trust affairs.[393] Fourth, personal rights held by a trustee are not eligible to be set off against debts irrelevant to trust business.[394] Fifth, if a security right over land X is held by a trustee for B (i.e., the beneficiary), the security right will not be extinguished even if the trustee acquires the ownership of X. In other words, B's beneficial right persists despite those two rights becoming vested in one person (i.e., the trustee).[395] This is, needless to say, aimed at protecting the beneficial interest. As these consequences illustrate, the Act, though not expressly accepted, virtually regards a trust fund as a segregated or separate patrimony/estate vis-à-vis the trustee's personal patrimony/estate.

§2. The Requirements

313. It must be noted that the trust fund enjoys the aforementioned protective effects only if the following requirements are met: for those rights which are registrable (e.g., land ownership and limited property right on land), they must be registered; if the rights held on trust exist in the form of securities on which personal rights are embedded, the fact that they form part of a trust fund must be specified by the relevant regulatory authority; if company shares or corporate bonds are held

388. Trust Act, Art. 9(1). The expression used in the official translation is "the property rights acquired by a trustee" (*see* http://law.moj.gov.tw). But as personal rights can also be held by a trustee, the expression causes serious confusion unless the term "property rights" is intended to encompass personal rights as well. Though possible, it is still misleading. This work adopts the terms "rights," "assets" or "trust fund" in order to avoid such uncertainty.
389. Trust Act, Art. 9(2).
390. Trust Act, Art. 10.
391. Trust Act, Art. 11.
392. Trust Act, Art. 12
393. Trust Act, Art. 12(1)(Proviso).
394. Trust Act, Art. 13.
395. Trust Act, Art. 14.

by a trustee, a notice must be given to the issuing company or corporate body;[396] for those rights that cannot be made public, the objects (money, chattels, etc.) held on trust should be kept separately.[397] These measures are mainly designed to enhance the noticeability of the rights held on trust, which, as a corollary, reduces the conflicts between trusts and third parties.

396. Trust Act, Art. 4(1)(2)(3).
397. Trust Act, Art. 24.

Chapter 4. Duties, Liabilities, and Powers of the Trustee

§1. The Duties

314. Once a trust relationship is established, the Act imposes upon the trustee some duties that must be maintained in the course of management of the trust. For reasons of space, the section only introduces five of the duties owed by trustees. The first duty enshrined in the Act is *the duty of care,*[398] which requires the trustee to manage the trust in accordance with the care a prudent administrator would exercise. Then who is the prudent administrator? It is generally submitted that those of identical occupation and position in the market fall within this category. In other words, an objective test is applied when deciding the degree of the duty. The trustee is also obliged to separate the trust fund from his own private assets and, if any, other trust funds.[399] *The duty to separate trust funds* is crucial in that it promotes certainty for third parties in the market to verify which assets held by the trustee are subject to the trust. The duty to separate trust funds is normally achieved by meeting the aforementioned requirements concerning the protective efficacy of the fund.

315. Following these two duties comes *the duty of non-delegation,*[400] a duty that prohibits the trustee from delegating the management of trust business to a third party. The rationale behind this is that the trustee in question is the very person that the settlor entrusts, thus any delegation would go against the settlor's intention. However, as trust affairs are becoming more and more diverse and complicated, it is virtually impossible for trustees to manage every single detail of their trust affairs. Thus, the law permits trustees to deviate from this duty and delegate part of their business, if and only if the power of delegation is given by the trust instrument, or if there arises an event where delegation is unavoidable.[401] The fourth duty to be mentioned is *the duty to make trust accounts*, a duty requiring the trustee to list trust assets and record any changes in the course of administration of the trust. This also serves to help beneficiaries know whether the trust business is being managed properly. The duty forms the foundation of the disclosure of information that may affect all interested parties of the trust.

316. The last and most important of all duties owed by a trustee is *the duty of loyalty or fiduciary duty*. This is a duty that compels the trustee to handle trust business to the exclusion of any personal interest (i.e., disinterestedly). What merits discussing are the two core-rules embedded in this duty: the no-conflict rule and the no-profit rule. The no-conflict rule prevents trustees from making any self-dealings with the assets they hold in the trustees' capacity.[402] This rule is, however, subject to three exceptions:[403] (1) if self-dealing is made with the written consent of the

398. Trust Act, Art. 22.
399. Trust Act, Art. 24.
400. Trust Act, Art. 25.
401. Trust Act, Art. 25 (proviso).
402. Trust Act, Art. 35.
403. Trust Act, Art. 35(1)(i)(ii)(iii).

beneficiary and at the market price; (2) if self-dealing is made through competing with other buyers at the market; and (3) if self-dealing is permitted by a court. As for the no-profit rule, this demands trustees not to procure any profits in the course of administration of trust.[404] Therefore, trustees are not allowed to obtain any commission (i.e., a bribe) from a contractor for choosing the latter to construct a building for the trust. In a similar vein, the trustees are strictly barred from selling information acquired in the course of management of a trust and earning money from it.

317. The net effect of all this is as follows: trustees must in principle act disinterestedly. The duty of loyalty as such may seem draconian, yet it can be justified considering that all rights are vested in trustees of whom the beneficial interest is divested: a mechanism is thus called for to perpetuate this deprivation of the interest.[405]

§2. The Liabilities

318. The aforementioned duties are preventative measures in their nature. However, they will not be useful unless supported by corrective measures, like two sides of a coin. The Act, by holding trustees liable for breach of the duties, corrects the damage caused to the trust. Article 23 of the Act states: trustees are obliged to pay pecuniary compensation for the loss suffered by the trust, or to restore the damage to its original condition, if it is provoked by trustees' improper management or breach of the purpose or terms of the trust. By the interaction of the duties and remedies, breaches are prevented and losses are recovered.

319. However, a question arises: what if the trustee commits a breach, but no loss befalls the trust, yet the trustee obtains profits from the breach? Most commonly, cases involve the trustee breaching the duty of loyalty. To illustrate, if a trustee breaches the no-conflict rule and obtains a trust asset through self-dealing, the trustee is still liable to return the asset to the trust despite having paid a reasonable price.[406] Similarly, if a trustee obtains commission (i.e., a bribe) from a contractor for choosing the latter to construct a building for the trust, or if the trustee receives rewards from a third party for offering the latter information acquired in the course of management of the trust, the trustee is required to disgorge the profits gained through the breach of the no-profit rule.[407] The remedy of disgorgement of profits performs a decisive role in diminishing the trustee's incentive to obtain any profits by breaching the duty of loyalty; this is so because he cannot defend himself on the basis that the trust suffers no loss; this not only promotes the preventative

404. Trust Act, Art. 34.
405. Unless they are one of the beneficiaries.
406. Trust Act, Art. 35(3).
407. The effect is not laid down in the Act. However, it should be identical to the case of breach of the no-conflict rule, for they are both elements of the duty of loyalty.

function of the duty, but also may trigger trustees to concentrate more on the appropriate execution of trust affairs than on exploiting the trust.

§3. The Rights

320. Having examined the duties and liabilities, we have found that rather draconian burdens are shouldered by trustees. Trustees, however, also have some rights. First, trustees are entitled to claim remuneration if they are corporate trustees that accept the trust as part of their business, or if the terms of the trust so provide.[408] Second, trustees are entitled to pay out of the trust fund any taxes, expenses, or debts incurred from managing the trust.[409] Third, if the trust's funds are not sufficient to cover the aforementioned taxes, expenses, or debts, trustees are capable of claiming that the beneficiary should pay for them.[410] Fourth, if a trustee makes a payment for the trust's taxes and expenses from his own assets,[411] he is conferred a right to obtain reimbursement from the trust fund, and his position is ranked above other trust creditors having only personal rights.[412] Fifth, unless the trustee's right of reimbursement is satisfied, he may refuse to bestow any benefits from the trust fund upon the beneficiary.[413] These five rights awarded to the trustee are, however, subject to one limitation, namely that the rights are not exercisable unless he or she has fully implemented any liability to compensate losses to the trust, recover dissipated trust funds or disgorge profits obtained.[414] This reflects the old English maxim of equity that he who wants to assert his rights must come to equity with clean hands.

---

408. Trust Act, Art. 38.
409. Trust Act, Art. 39(1).
410. Trust Act, Art. 40(1).
411. Please note that "debts" are excluded.
412. Trust Act, Art. 39(2).
413. Trust Act, Art. 41.
414. Trust Act, Art. 44.

Chapter 5. Rights of the Beneficiary

§1. Beneficiary's Right to Beneficial Interest

321. Once a trust is created, the trustee must act disinterestedly, and manage the trust solely for the benefit of the beneficiary. Trustees are, therefore, under an obligation, *inter alia*, to bestow beneficial interest out of trust funds, and only from the fund, upon their beneficial owner(s).[415] This means that the beneficiary of a trust is entitled to the beneficial interest upon the creation of the trust unless otherwise stipulated in the trust instrument.[416] Furthermore, the settlor is, after the trust is created, not permitted to change the beneficiary to another person, alter the content of the beneficial interest, or terminate the trust unless the settlor reserves those rights in the trust instrument or the beneficiary consents to it.[417] It can be easily perceived that the limitations on the part of the settlor exist to protect the beneficiary's expectation of receiving the benefits of the trust.

322. Beneficial interest is taken from trust fund, such that the fund is the fountain of the interest distributed to beneficiaries. Protection of the fund thus matters. The law achieves this goal in three ways. First, trust fund is protected by those aforementioned effects given to the fund itself. Second, the fund is secured by imposing upon trustees some protective duties preventing the fund from being co-mingled with or transferred to their own personal assets, namely, the duty to separate trust funds and the duty of loyalty. Third, a beneficiary is entitled to rescind the disposition made between the trustee and *a third party* in breach of trust (the so-called third-party effect).[418] This last right needs further elaboration.

§2. The Beneficiary's Right of Rescission

323. The right of rescission held by a beneficiary, being a remedy against a third party,[419] assists him to recover trust assets from third parties. Trust funds thus can remain protected. The right to rescind a disposition made in breach of trust is however subject to the following three requirements.[420] First, the right is only exercisable in court, i.e., an illicit disposition made by a trustee can only be rescinded by

415. Trust Act, Art. 30.
416. Trust Act, Art. 17.
417. Trust Act, Art. 3.
418. Trust Act, Art. 18(1): "The beneficiary of a trust shall have the right to apply to the court for revocation of the disposal of trust property, if the property has been disposed of by the trustee in violation of the stated purpose of the trust. If there is more than one beneficiary, the motion for revocation may be filed by any one of the beneficiaries."
419. This right, though not exactly identical, is more or less similar to *Actio Pauliana* of the Roman law.
420. Trust Act, Art. 18(2)(i)(iii). Art. 18 stipulates that "[t]he right to apply for revocation as provided in the preceding paragraph may be exercised only in any one of the following situations: (i) The trust property is a property right which requires registration and such trust registration has been duly completed … . (iii) The trust property is a property right other than those provided in the

a court order. Second, if the illicitly disposed assets are registrable, they must be registered before the disposition. Third, for those non-registrable assets, the beneficiary must prove that the third-party disponee knew or should have known that the trustee wrongfully alienated the fund to the disponee, i.e., the beneficiary can assert the right of rescission against all third parties save bona fide disponees.

324. The second requirement somehow causes a problem. What matters in exercising the right of rescission is whether the third party actually *knew or should have known of the breach*, not the registration itself. While registration does inform us of whom the parties to the disposition are, and thus offers the third party an opportunity to check the trust instrument to see whether or not the trustee is disposing of the trust fund in breach of trust, it is neither practical nor realistic in a commercial market for third parties in the market to read through the trust instrument in every transaction. Trustees are in many cases allowed to invest the fund, and third parties normally believe that trustees are empowered to alienate it. The upshot is that, in the case of breach of trust, the technique of registration cannot be used as a means to deem all people in the market as *mala fide* transferees. The second requirement should be aligned with the third one: the beneficiary is entitled to exercise the right of rescission against all disponees save those bona fide purchasers without notice of the breach.

325. One final question emerges: can we regard the beneficiary's right *over trust funds* as proprietary in its nature on the basis of the beneficiary's right of rescission? The answer to this question should surely be negative, for there would be no need to rescind the disposition if the beneficiary's right were proprietary; the beneficiary could simply assert his property right without the aid of rescission![421] To conclude, while it may be possible to depict a beneficiary's right as a proprietary right in common-law jurisdictions,[422] it can hardly be the case in Taiwan. As far as

preceding two subparagraphs and the transferee (or the subsequent transferee) knew or should have known that the trustee had disposed of the property against the stated purpose of the trust."

421. Wu Ying-Chieh, *East Asian Trusts at the Crossroads*, 10 National Taiwan U. L. Rev. 79, 107 (2015).

422. It is not uncommon to hear the view that the common-law trust is predicated on the concept of dual ownership: one at law and the other in equity. But this view is extremely doubtful in that the concept of dual ownership is rejected by most of the current authoritative common-law scholars. For more details, *see* F.H. Lawson, *A Common Lawyer Looks at the Civil Law* 203 (Michigan Law School 1955), William Swadling, *Property: General Principles, in English Private Law* 217, 272–274 (Andrew Burrow ed., Oxford Univ. Press 2d ed. 2008), Tony Honoré, *On Fitting Trusts into Civil Law Jurisdiction*, 27 Oxford L. S. Research Paper (2008/09), SSRN: http://ssrn.com/abstract=1270179, Ben McFarlane, *The Structure of Property Law* 26 (Hart Publishing 2008). Moreover, the concept is not viable under the civil law notion of ownership. For more details, *see* Wu Ying-Chieh, *Trust Law in South Korea: Developments and Challenges, in Trust Law in Asian Civil Law Jurisdictions: A Comparative Analysis* 46, 57 (Lusina Ho & Rebecca Lee eds., Oxford Univ. Press 2013).

the Taiwanese law of trust is concerned, the beneficiary does not hold any proprietary interest over trust funds; he simply has a personal right to demand the trustee to bestow trust benefits upon him (i.e., the beneficiary).[423]

423. However, problems still remain. More solid theoretical grounds should be given for the insolvency effect and third-party effect. Otherwise the personal right approach would become less persuasive. For reasons of space, the issue will be dealt with elsewhere.

Chapter 6. Termination of the Trust

§1. Grounds for Termination

326. The life of a trust begins from the settlor's manifestation of an intention to create it (i.e., via a trust contract, will, or self-declaration of trust). And we must not forget that trust funds are to be utilized for a specified beneficiary or charitable purpose. The truth is that managing a trust fund for a beneficiary is itself a purpose (i.e., a private purpose). Therefore, we are able to imagine two possibilities for a trust to be terminated: one is termination based on the settlor's *intention* (an intention-based termination) and the other is termination grounded on whether the trust's *purpose* is still realizable (a purpose-based termination). Reflecting the twofold aspects, the law stipulates that the settlor is capable of terminating the trust if he is also the sole beneficiary of the trust, unless otherwise provided for in the trust instrument.[424] Where the settlor is not the sole beneficiary, he can only terminate the trust if the right of termination is exercised jointly with the other beneficiary.[425] Moreover, it is fully possible for a settlor to list the grounds for termination in the trust instrument, and the trust terminates once the grounds are realized.[426] It should be noted that the beneficiary alone cannot terminate the trust, and thus there is no *Saunders v. Vautier*[427] Rule in Taiwan.[428] Finally, a trust also terminates if the purpose of it are accomplished or impossible to reach.[429] On the other hand, a trust may not be terminated merely because the settlor or trustee dies, becomes insolvent, or loses legal capacity.[430] Moreover, in a system without *the rule against the remoteness of vesting* (i.e., a sub-rule of the rules against perpetuity), a trust, either for private or public purpose, can last for good. However, considering that assets may possibly be carved out of the market once they are held under a trust, a private purpose trust should be made subject to the rule.[431] But a charitable purpose trust would be exempted from this rule under utilitarian or communitarian considerations, namely that charitable trusts are worth lasting forever.

§2. Residual Funds

327. There may exist residual funds at the time a trust is terminated. They surely need to be vested in someone entitled to receive them. The first candidate to whom

424. Trust Act, Art. 63(1).
425. Trust Act, Art. 64(1).
426. Trust Act, Art. 62.
427. (1841) 4 Beav 115.
428. However, the settlor may die or become incapacitated, and it is virtually impossible for the settlor to terminate a trust in a testamentary trust. Thus, it may be advisable for Taiwanese law to import the rule in *Saunders v. Vautier*.
429. Trust Act, Art. 62.
430. Trust Act, Art. 8.
431. A period of 125 years is applied in England under the Perpetuities and Accumulations Act 2009. Thus, any beneficial interest designed to be vested later than 125 years from the creation of the trust is void. The English approach may offer Taiwanese law a good model to refer to.

the residual funds are to be transferred is the beneficiary who is entitled to the whole benefits at the time of termination.[432] If there is no such beneficiary, the residual funds are returned to the settlor or his successor.[433] Here we find a gap existing between the termination of trust and the vesting of residual funds in the aforementioned people. To elaborate, these people are obviously not beneficiaries of any trust since the time they are entitled to receive the residual funds comes after the trust is terminated. And the original trustee should be discharged from the position since the trust is already terminated. As a consequence, no one is, technically speaking, obliged to transfer the residual funds to the people mentioned above. The law needs to create a fiction to deal with this: the creation of a new trust for them. A new trust, therefore, arises *by operation of law* (i.e., a statutory trust), and the trustee at the time of termination, being the trustee of the newly created trust, continues to be liable to hold and transfer the residual funds for the benefit of those entitled (i.e., the new beneficiaries).[434] The gap is sealed.

328. However, the rules mentioned in the preceding paragraph cannot be expected to function properly in charitable trusts that do not have any specific beneficiaries. The doctrine of *cy-pres* is instead applied to them. The residual funds of a charitable trust would be used for another purpose similar to the initial charitable purpose, or they can be transferred to a charitable legal entity or a charitable trust with a purpose close to the original one.[435] The doctrine of *cy-pres*, coupled with the exemption from the rule against the remoteness of vesting, makes charitable trusts de facto immortal.

432. Trust Act, Art. 65(1)(i).
433. Trust Act, Art. 65(1)(ii).
434. Trust Act, Art. 66.
435. Trust Act, Art. 79.

Part V. Trust and Fiduciary Mechanisms

329. Roman law had two forms of fiduciary mechanism (i.e., *fiducia*): the *fiducia cum amico* and the *fiducia cum creditore*.[436] Though both types of *fiducia* were accepted and employed in the classical period of Roman history, they became obsolete and were not adopted by the Justinian code in the fifth century. Taiwan has not recognized and transplanted the Roman *fiducia*. However, this does not denote Taiwanese law knows nothing about fiduciary mechanism—it does have one that is imported from the common-law tradition: Trust (for more details please *see* Part IV Trust).

436. For more details, *see* Nicolas Malumian, *Trusts in Latin America* 5, 6 (Oxford Univ. Press 2009).

Part VI. Security

Chapter 1. Security in Immovable Property

330. The Taiwan Civil Code provides three types of security rights[437] in immovable property that also normally exist in other jurisdictions: mortgage, pledge, and lien. Mortgage is only applicable to immovable property, whereas pledge and lien are only applicable to movable property. Notably, the concept of a "charge" is not a type of security right in Taiwan.

331. However, under the Torrens system, mortgages usually operate as a charge because, once registered, a mortgage does not require the holder of the mortgaged property to transfer possession of that property to the mortgagee anymore. As the Torrens system renders registered property interests indefeasible, any subsequent transfer of the mortgaged properties will be subject to the mortgage, if it is registered. Therefore, the transfer of possession as a way for the mortgagee to protect his or her interest in the mortgaged property is not necessary anymore. As the mortgagor is permitted to possess such property, it also facilitates the mortgagee's use of such property. As such, the traditional distinction between mortgage and charge—that is, a charge does not require the transfer of possession whereas a mortgage does[438]—does not exist anymore under Taiwan's Torrens system. In other countries that have adopted the Torrens system, such as Singapore, the distinction between a charge and a mortgage is likewise unclear for the same reason.[439]

332. Chapter 4 of Part I of this volume introduces a special type of security right that was derived from the customary law in the Chinese agricultural economy—*dian*. Like a traditional mortgage, the owner of land can create a *dian* under which the right to possess such land will be transferred to the *dian*-holder in return for a premium. Accordingly, the *dian*-maker has the right to redeem the land anytime during the term of such *dian*. Unlike a mortgage, however, the mechanism for redeeming property and the remedies available if such property is not redeemed

437. *See also* Part I and Part IV.

438. In the UK, this terminological distinction between mortgage and charge has also receded in importance over the decades. *See* Kevin Gray & Susan Francis Gray, *Elements of Land Law* 694 (Oxford Univ. Press 5th ed. 2009). For discussions based on the traditional distinction between mortgage and charge, *see, e.g.*, *Santley v. Wilde* [1899] 2 Ch 474 per Lindley LJ; *English Scottish and Australian Bank Ltd v. Phillips* (1937) 57 CLR 302.

439. Sook Yee Tan, Tang Hang Wu & Kelvin F.K. Low, *Tan Sook Yee's Principles of Singapore Land Law* 568 (LexisNexis 2010).

are different. For example, the *dian*-holder is entitled to be registered under Taiwan's Torrens system as the owner of the property the *dian* was created over if the *dian*-maker fails to redeem the property after a certain period of time. This is different from the procedure for judicial sale found commonly in the enforcement of mortgages. For a detailed discussion of *dian*, please *see* Chapter 4 of Part I of the volume.

§1. Privileges, Liens, Charges

I. Relationship among Privileges, Lien, and Charges

333. Privileges, as a type of security right, are not separately provided for under the Taiwan Civil Code. Rather, privileges exist as a type of statutory right, depending on contemporary policy considerations, that awards priority (e.g., statutory lien) to certain parties in certain types of legal relationships. With respect to charges, as stated earlier, it is not a type of security right in Taiwan. As such, privileges are not confined to one specific area of law in Taiwan but are found under several special areas of law (e.g., the Maritime Law in Taiwan). They also exist as an ancillary right attached to other legal rights under the Taiwan Civil Code. Notably, the German Civil Code adopts the same approach. For example, where the shipping carrier is entitled to specific performance against the charterer who fails to pay service fees, he or she may select to exercise the lien as part of remedy, over the charterer's cargos on the ship. In comparison, France's and Japan's civil laws view privileges as a general type of security right and provide a set of separate rules to govern privileges. In any case, privileges provide a form of priority for certain interest holders to strengthen their contractual or proprietary interests.

334. Generally speaking, three types of privileges exist under Taiwan's Civil Code and other special laws: lien, right of first refusal, and the right of priority claim. They may co-exist in one legal relationship, such as in a tenant-landlord relationship. For example, the tenant under a lease, who has constructed residential property thereon, is entitled to the right of first refusal if the landlord wants to sell the underlying land.[440] Where the tenant fails to pay rent, the landlord is entitled to a lien so that he may retain the movable properties that the tenant places on the real property as a security against the rent in arrears.[441] The nature of lien is a right in rem, as provided by the Taiwan Civil Code Book 3 Chapter 9 "Lien." In comparison, the nature of the rights of first refusal and of priority claim is a contractual right, although sometimes the legislature has made the right of refusal a right in rem—*see, e.g.*, Article 426-2 of the Taiwan Civil Code and Article 104 of the Land Act. The Taiwan Civil Code lacks general provisions concerning the right of first refusal and the right of priority.

---

440. Taiwan Civil Code, Art. 426-2.
441. Taiwan Civil Code, Art. 445.

II. Lien

335. Lien is the right of a creditor to retain personal property of a debtor if the debtor defaults on payment and if the personal property is associated with the contractual relationship underlying the creditor's claim.[442] Lien is provided for varying types of contractual relationships. In addition to the landlord's lien over the tenant's personal property, the landowner has the right to retain the personal property or animals of any person who trespasses unto his or her land, whether intentionally or by accident, for the purpose of claiming compensation for any damage that results from such trespass.

336. Also, the proprietor of a hotel is entitled to retain the luggage or other personal property of the guests if the guests have yet to pay any fee incurred in relation to lodging, food, services, and disbursements.[443] Lien is also available to parties in some other legal relations, such as the right of shipping carriers to retain cargo in default of payment,[444] the right of forwarding agents to retain goods in default of payment,[445] and the right of persons who have found lost property that carries a reward to retain such property in default of receiving such an award.[446]

337. Because lien is also a security right in movable property, this volume discusses it in the context of movable property in §2 of Chapter 2 in Part VI.

III. The Right of First Refusal

338. The right of first refusal gives its holder a call option to purchase property from the owner before the owner transfers it to a third party. No provision about a general right of first refusal exists within the Taiwan Civil Code. Nevertheless, this right typically exists as an ancillary right to certain property or contractual relations. It is a right in personam rather than a right in rem.

339. For example, the Land Act gives the right of first refusal to the holders of *superficies*, *dian*, and leases when the owner intends to sell the underlying land.[447] The owner is required to serve a notice to the holders of such rights and can transfer the land to a third party only after the right holder fails to exercise the right within ten days.[448] Similarly, in a lease of land for the purpose of constructing a residential building, the lessee is entitled to exercise his or her right of first refusal if the lessor

442. Taiwan Civil Code, Art. 928.
443. Taiwan Civil Code, Art. 612.
444. Taiwan Civil Code, Art. 647.
445. Taiwan Civil Code, Art. 662.
446. Taiwan Civil Code, Art. 805.
447. The Land Act, Art. 104.
448. Article 919 of the Civil Code repeats the right of first refusal provided for *dian*-holders.

intends to sell the land. Similarly, the lessor is required to serve a ten-day notice to the lessee and can only transfer the land to a third party if the lessee does not exercise the right within ten days.[449]

IV. The Right of Priority Claim

340. The right of priority gives the right holder a priority over other creditors in order to protect his or her contractual interests. For example, Taiwan's Maritime Law grants certain parties the right of priority over the value of the ship in relation to certain types of claims (e.g., claims by crew members for unpaid salary).[450] The nature of this right in Maritime Law, according to the majority view, is a right in rem.[451]

341. Under the Taiwan Civil Code, the right of priority claim also exists in the form of a statutory mortgage in some contexts. For example, a building contractor is entitled to request for the registration of a mortgage in his or her name against real property that he or she is contracted to work on (e.g., to provide repair work). This statutory mortgage, once registered, is superior to any other mortgage registered earlier to the extent of the increased value of the property as a result of the contractor's work.[452]

§2. Mortgage

I. Concept and General Features

342. The Taiwan Civil Code provides two types of mortgages: the general mortgage and the line-of-credit mortgage. A general mortgage is defined as a right that grants the mortgagee priority to satisfy the mortgage claim from the sale proceeds of the mortgaged property without the need to transfer possession of such property from the debtor or a third party.[453] The line-of-credit mortgage was introduced by the 2010 amendment to the Taiwan Civil Code, although for years it had been recognized as a valid type of mortgage. This new type of mortgage allows parties to stipulate the maximum amount of credit line in the loan contract without requiring the borrower/mortgagor to borrow the full loaned amount at the outset. In this way, the line-of-credit mortgage secures an uncertain amount of debt, part of which may not have happened yet but may happen in the future. This differs from the general mortgage, which requires the underlying debt to be ascertained when the general mortgage is entered into.

---

449. Taiwan Civil Code, Art. 426-2.
450. The Maritime Law, Art. 24.
451. Zhang-Hua Yin, Maritime Law Cases and Materials (2008), available at: http://www.lawtw.com/article.php?template=article_content&area=free_browse&parent_path=,1,2008,&job_id=58365&article_category_id=1513&article_id=28198.
452. Taiwan Civil Code, Art. 513.
453. Taiwan Civil Code, Art. 860.

343. Under Taiwan's Torrens system, the mortgagor does not need to transfer possession of the mortgaged property to the mortgagee for a mortgage to be legally effective. What this means is that mortgages in Taiwan are effectively charges, which are not formally recognized under the Taiwan Civil Code as a type of security right. As mentioned, this arrangement is common in other Torrens systems, which render titles indefeasible once registered. For example, under Singapore's Torrens system, mortgages also operate as charges and the mortgagor does not have to transfer possession of the mortgaged property to the mortgagee.[454]

344. Also, the loans underlying a mortgage cannot be separately transferred to a third party in Taiwan. The mortgagee/creditor has to assign the secured loans, if necessary, together with the mortgage. Additionally, mortgages cannot be the object of another mortgage as this would complicate the transaction and render the enforcement of either mortgage difficult.[455]

345. It should be noted that the object of mortgage is not limited to ownership. One can create a mortgage against *superficies*, agricultural rights, and *dian* in the form of a general mortgage or a line-of-credit mortgage.[456]

Figure 7 shows that mortgage has been widely used.

Figure 7 Number of Registration Filing, Mortgage, 2005–2020

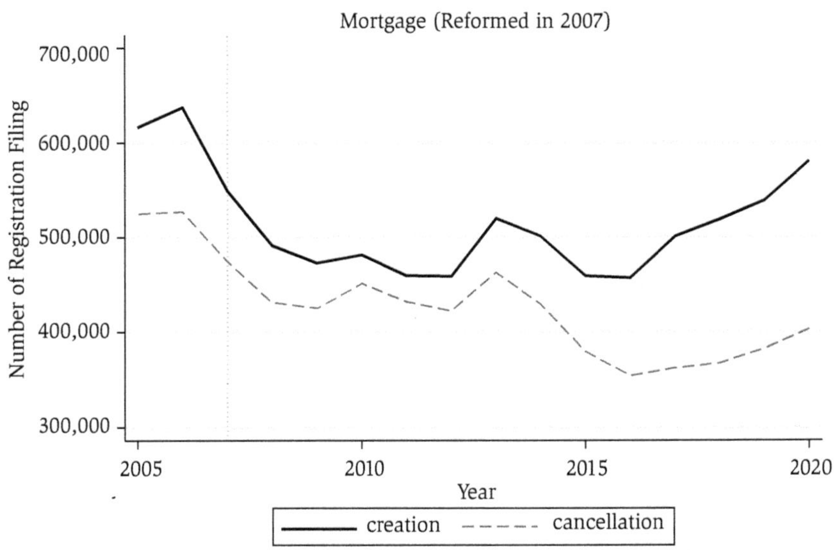

Data source: Statistical Yearbook of the Ministry of the Interior, Taiwan.
Graph created by the authors: Dotted vertical line shows the year of reform.

454. Sook Yee Tan, Tang Hang Wu & Kelvin FK Low, *Tan Sook Yee's Principles of Singapore Land Law* 568 (LexisNexis 2010).
455. Taiwan Civil Code, Art. 870.
456. Taiwan Civil Code, Arts. 882, 883.

II. Scope of the Interests under a Mortgage

346. To prevent disputes, the Taiwan Civil Code provides a set of comprehensive rules to define the scope of the interests under a mortgage. The object of mortgage includes not only the mortgaged property but also its natural profits that are separable from the mortgaged property, as well as any accessories, ancillary rights, or substitutes for the mortgaged property.[457] What is covered and secured by the mortgage includes the loan principal, as well as regular payments of interest, penalties for late payment penalties and the interest payable thereon, and the costs of enforcement, if any.[458]

347. One breakthrough made by the 2007 amendment to the Taiwan Civil Code concerns the line-of-credit mortgage: the underlying loan covered by the mortgage need not be ascertained and quantified at the time of creating the line-of-credit mortgage. However, the amount loaned has to be ascertained at some point. The Taiwan Civil Code provides a list of events that requires such amounts to be ascertained immediately should they materialize. For example, if the creditor/mortgagee refuses to continue to provide such credits, the debtor/mortgagor is entitled to request the creditor/mortgagee to ascertain the amount loaned immediately so that the unpaid debts can be determined and settled as soon as possible.[459]

348. Moreover, as the ownership of land and the ownership of buildings are separate and distinct in Taiwan and can be owned by different persons, mortgages may be created against both the land and building or against only one of them. Where the land and building belong to the same owner, the legal relationship is manageable in terms of mortgage enforcement. However, if the land and the building belongs to or subsequently belongs to different owners, the mortgagee may face difficulty in enforcing the mortgage. Taiwan's Civil Code, therefore, provides a number of rules to prevent the potential problems caused in such a scenario.

349. For example, if the land and the building thereon are both owned by the mortgagor but only one of them (e.g., the building) is mortgaged, the Taiwan Civil Code stipulates that if the mortgaged property is sold as a result of the enforcement of such mortgage, the buyer of the mortgaged property (i.e., the building) will receive a *superficies* in respect of the other property (i.e., the land on which the building was erected on).[460] In this way, the buyer is entitled to continue to utilize the land subject to the new terms to be agreed upon between the buyer and the landowner.

350. There are also cases in which the owner of mortgaged land, after creating such a mortgage, subsequently erects buildings on the mortgaged land. In such cases, when the mortgagee exercises the right to sell, the court, if necessary, may

457. Taiwan Civil Code, Arts. 862, 862-1, 863, and 864.
458. Taiwan Civil Code, Art. 861.
459. Taiwan Civil Code, Art. 881-12.
460. Taiwan Civil Code, Art. 876.

order the buildings to be sold as well in order to prevent the over-fragmentation of the ownership of building and land. The proceeds of the sale of such buildings, however, shall not be used to satisfy the mortgagee's claims.[461]

III. Altering the Priority of Multiple Mortgages

351. If multiple mortgages exist on the same property, their priority is determined according to the order of their registration. After the creation of a mortgage, the owner of the mortgaged property is allowed to create other types of property rights, such as *superficies* or agriculture rights, to better facilitate the use of property. Similarly, these rights in rem that are subsequently created are subjected to the existing mortgage. If the existing mortgage is affected, the mortgagee is entitled to request a court to order an injunction and/or extinguish the property rights that were subsequently created.[462]

352. The 2007 amendment to the Taiwan Civil Code introduced a new mechanism that allows multiple mortgagees of mortgaged property to alter the priority of their mortgages amongst themselves. Through this mechanism, one mortgagee may assign his right of priority to another mortgagee or waive his priority in favor of a mortgagee of lesser priority. The mortgagee can also waive his priority in favor of all mortgagees of lesser priority (Article 870-1 of the Taiwan Civil Code). However, such an assignment or waiver of priority will not take effect unless it is registered. Prior to the registration, the mortgagee shall notify the debtor, the mortgagor, and any other joint mortgagor. If there exists any guarantor whose rights may be affected by such alteration of priority amongst the multiple mortgages, the alteration is not binding unless the consent of such a guarantor has been obtained (Article 870-2 of the Taiwan Civil Code). It should be noted that this mechanism also exists in German and Japanese property law. As a matter of fact, the alteration of priority order was not uncommon in practice in Taiwan before the 2007 amendment.

353. For instance, the alteration of the order of priority among multiple mortgages is common practice in capital markets and the banking industry. Institutional lenders from time to time have to adjust the order of priority between existing mortgages so as to better tailor their offerings. Conventionally, this alteration could be done through private agreement between new lenders and existing creditors. Now a statutory basis is provided for such alterations under the Taiwan Civil Code.

IV. Enforcement

354. There are two ways in which mortgages are enforced. The first is through a judicial sale. The mortgagee who has not been repaid upon the maturity of the

461. Taiwan Civil Code, Art. 877.
462. Taiwan Civil Code, Art. 866.

underlying loans may apply to court to foreclose the mortgaged property through an auction.[463] Second, the mortgagee may enter into an agreement with the mortgagor to acquire the mortgaged property or dispose of it by any means other than a judicial auction on the condition that the agreed method would not affect the interests of other mortgagees.[464]

355. Prior to enforcement, if any act of the mortgagor is likely to cause a reduction in the value of the mortgaged property, the mortgagee may demand the mortgagor to cease the act. Under urgent circumstances, the mortgagee may even make a necessary disposition to safeguard his interests.[465] Any cost incurred for such an action shall be borne by all mortgagees, as the case may be, and the mortgagor shall be given priority over all other existing mortgage claims because such disposition preserved the value of the mortgaged property for the benefit of all mortgagees.

463. Taiwan Civil Code, Art. 873.
464. Taiwan Civil Code, Art. 878.
465. Taiwan Civil Code, Art. 871.

Chapter 2. Security in Movable Property

§1. PLEDGES

I. Creation

356. The pledge, an ancient form of security right, is defined as a property right over movable property, which requires the delivery of possession from the debtor (i.e., pledgor) to the creditor (i.e., pledgee), and the latter enjoys priority vis-à-vis the former's other personal creditors should the former become insolvent.[466] Thus, pledge is a possessory security right, and the transfer of possession of the thing to the pledgee is a vital element of it. It is not permitted for the pledgor to take possession on behalf of the pledgee,[467] for this would virtually remove the hallmark of this regime. As a corollary of this, two steps are in principle required for the creation of a pledge: apart from the mutual consents (i.e., real agreement) concluded by the debtor and the creditor on the latter acquiring a pledge in the former's moveable property, it also requires that possession of the thing itself be transferred to the creditor (i.e., pledgee). This connotes that a pledge does not come into being unless the subject-matter is possessed by the creditor/pledgee.[468] Since a pledge involves the pledgee retaining possession of the property, some rights and duties on the part of the pledgee ensue. We shall look at them below.

II. The Pledgee's Rights and Duties Following from Possession

357. As explored in the previous paragraph, the pledgee procures the possession of the movable property offered to him by his pledgor as security for the loan. This implies that the subject-matter of the security is *in the hands of*: (1) a person who is *not* an owner of it; (2) but *is vested* with a proprietary interest over it. The law, by taking these two aspects into account, generates the following three effects. First, since the pledgee only holds a security right, he is not an owner of the pledged thing; the standard duty of care is imposed upon and is thus expected to be exercised by the pledgee when possessing the thing pledged.[469] Moreover, the pledgee is prohibited from using or leasing the thing without the consent of the pledgor.[470] The first effect obviously protects the pledgor's (i.e., the owner's) reversionary interest in that it helps the thing pledged maintain its condition when returned. Second, the pledgee is entitled to acquire any fruits derived from the pledged thing unless otherwise provided in the agreement.[471] The fruits so collected shall be applied to discharge the following in order: (1) collateral costs required for possession and execution; (2) any interests arising from the capital money borrowed; (3)

466. Taiwan Civil Code, Art. 884.
467. Taiwan Civil Code, Art. 885(2).
468. Taiwan Civil Code, Art. 885(1).
469. Taiwan Civil Code, Art. 888(1).
470. Taiwan Civil Code, Art. 888(2).
471. Taiwan Civil Code, Art. 889.

the capital money itself.[472] The second effect promotes the interests of the pledgee by enabling him to use the proceeds from the pledged thing for the discharge of the debt. Third, if the thing pledged is likely to be perishable or there is an obvious depreciation in its value sufficient to prejudice the rights of the pledgee, the pledgee may sell the thing pledged by auction and keep the proceeds from sale in place of the thing pledged.[473] This third effect is aimed at extending the life of the pledge which would otherwise be extinguished or lose value for the pledgee.

III. Extinction

A. Extinction by Execution

358. It goes without saying that the pledgor can recover the thing pledged by performing his obligation (i.e., paying the debt) owed to the pledgee. However, once he defaults, protections for security rights are activated, entitling the pledgee to sell the thing at auction[474] and to enjoy priority[475] vis-à-vis the pledgor's other personal creditors. This means that the pledgee is capable of satisfying his debt prior to other creditors. It should be noted that it is fully possible for both parties to agree that the pledgee acquires ownership of the thing pledged once the pledgor fails to repay the debt.[476] But this does not mean the pledgee is qualified to obtain any windfall if the value of it exceeds that of the debt owed; the pledgee must reimburse the residual value to the pledgor.[477] Apart from the aforementioned two routes, the pledgee is also allowed to dispose of the thing and satisfy his debt from the proceeds arising from the disposition; this is however subject to an agreement concluded between the parties.[478] The pledge is extinguished once it is executed by any of the routes mentioned above.

359. Mention must be made of the following two questions: first, to what extent do the proceeds flowing from the disposition of the pledged thing cover the pledgor's debt? Second, what if a new movable property is substituted for the thing pledged at the beginning?[479] The answer to the first question is that they secure the original debt, its interest, penalties, cost of preserving the pledged thing, cost of executing the pledge, and damages for any injury caused by a defect of the thing

---

472. Taiwan Civil Code, Art. 890(2).
473. Taiwan Civil Code, Art. 892(1).
474. The pledgee must inform the pledgor of this (Taiwan Civil Code, Art. 894).
475. Taiwan Civil Code, Art. 893(1).
476. Taiwan Civil Code, Art. 893(2).
477. Taiwan Civil Code, Arts. 893(2), 873-1(2).
478. Taiwan Civil Code, Arts. 895, 878.
479. For example, the pledged thing is destroyed by a third party, and the pledgor receives an identical good or monetary compensation from the tortfeasor.

pledged.[480] As for the second question, the law applies the doctrine of real subrogation and prescribes that any rights or things substituted consist of the subject-matter as the pledge.[481]

B. Extinction on Other Grounds

360. We have seen in the preceding section three illustrations in which a pledge is extinguished by the pledgee's right to execute the security once the pledgor defaults on his obligation. However, pledges can also be extinguished on other grounds. Three occasions merit our attention. First, a pledge is extinguished once its subject-matter is destroyed or perishes.[482] Second, a pledge is extinguished if the debt owed to the pledgee is discharged. The pledgee in this instance is obliged to return the thing pledged to either the pledgor or someone entitled to receive it.[483] Third, since the primary feature of a pledge is the pledgee's possession of the thing pledged, a pledge shall be extinguished once the pledgee returns it to the pledgor despite the debt still being outstanding. In this situation, any reservation intended to preserve the efficacy of the pledge is ineffective,[484] for it would deprive the key feature of the pledge that cannot be dispensed with: possession of the pledged thing. However, the law makes an exception to this consequence if the pledgee loses his possession unintentionally: the law gives him two years to recover the thing, otherwise, the pledge comes to an end.[485]

§2. Lien

I. Creation

A. A Non-consensual Security Right

361. A lien is defined as a property right, arising by operation of law, over movable and tangible property, which accords to the creditor (i.e., lienee) a right to *retain* the property already given by the debtor if the latter (i.e., lienor) defaults his obligation and the relevant debt and property are connected.[486] An archetypal example of lien can be found in a case where an auto repair shop exercises a repairer's lien by retaining a vehicle in its possession pending payment of its repair charges. Four elements need explaining. First, a lien is a security right not created by the parties' mutual consents, but generated *by operation of law*: a passive right

480. Taiwan Civil Code, Art. 887(1).
481. Taiwan Civil Code, Art. 899(2). Therefore, the identical goods or money given by the tortfeasor form the new subject-matter of the pledge.
482. Unless there is a substitute; in this case the doctrine of real subrogation applies—the pledge survives. Taiwan Civil Code, Art. 899(1).
483. Taiwan Civil Code, Art. 896.
484. Taiwan Civil Code, Art. 897.
485. Taiwan Civil Code, Art. 898.
486. Taiwan Civil Code, Art. 928.

to retain the property that is already given to the creditor. Second, it is confined to the case of movable and "*tangible*" property: physically non-possessory property cannot be the subject-matter of a lien. Third, as this illustration shows, there must be a connection between the debt (i.e., repair charges) and the thing (i.e., vehicle) held by the creditor. However, there is an exception to this connection rule: where the creditor's possession of the thing in question is given in the course of a regular business relationship with the debtor. In this case, the law deems a connection between the debt and the thing involved.[487] For example, if auto repair shop X regularly fixes broken taxies belonging to taxi company Y, X is then able to retain Y's taxi for the repair charges arising from another taxi of Y's. Fourth, a lien is generated when the payment of the debt is due. But an exception applies. Suppose auto repair shop X promises its customer Y that Y can test the fixed car for three days before paying the repair charges. Even so, X is entitled to retain the car if Y becomes insolvent on the date X would transfer possession of the car to Y.[488] The rule, by anticipating Y's default, protects X's interests by according to X a right to retain the thing (i.e., lien) in advance.

B. Obstacles

362. An apparently established lien might be defeated should the following three events occur. First, if possession of the thing is obtained through a tortious act, a lien does not arise.[489] This happens in the case where a thief retains the property for the repair charges he or she paid. A lien is, therefore negated, and the owner can recover the thing held by the thief. Second, if the lienee knows or should have known the subject-matter does not belong to the lienor when the possession of it is transferred, a lien does not arise.[490] Last but not least, if the lienee knows from the outset that a third party has a proprietary interest (other than ownership) over the thing given, the former cannot assert his right to retain against the latter.[491]

II. Lienee's Rights and Duties Arising from Possession

363. As with the case of a pledge, the subject-matter of the security is *in the hands of:* (1) a person who is *not* an owner of it; (2) but *is vested* a proprietary interest over it. Therefore, the three effects arising from these aspects in the case of a pledge are also applied, *mutatis mutandis*, to a lien. But the three consequences need elaborating. First, since the lienee only holds a security right, a duty of care is imposed upon him while possessing the thing subject to the lien.[492] Furthermore, the lienee is not allowed to use or lease the thing in question without the consent of

487. Taiwan Civil Code, Art. 929.
488. Taiwan Civil Code, Art. 931(1).
489. Taiwan Civil Code, Art. 928(2).
490. Taiwan Civil Code, Art. 928(2).
491. Taiwan Civil Code, Art. 932-1.
492. Taiwan Civil Code, Arts. 933, 888(1).

the lienor.[493] The first effect is aimed at securing the lienor's (i.e., the owner's) reversionary interest in that it promotes the maintenance of the condition of the thing subject to the lien. Second, the lienee is entitled to acquire any fruits derived from the thing unless otherwise provided in the agreement.[494] The fruits so collected shall be applied to discharge the following debts in order: (1) collateral costs required for possession and execution; (2) any interest arising from the capital money borrowed; and (3) the money owed itself.[495] Third, if the thing subject to the lien is likely to deteriorate, or there is obvious depreciation in its value enough to cause damage to the lienee, the lienee may sell the thing by auction and keep the proceeds as the object of the lien.[496]

III. Extinction

A. Extinction by Execution

364. A lien is extinguished once the debtor (i.e., lienor) repays the debt owed to the creditor (i.e., lienee). However, if the former defaults on payment, the latter can detain the whole thing (if it is not divisible) even if the value of the thing exceeds that of the money owed.[497] A creditor who has not received payment may set a reasonable time limit of at least one month, notify the debtor and declare that if the debt is not paid within the time limit, payment will be taken out of the thing retained.[498] This shows that a lienee does not enjoy an immediate right to sell the property. Execution is only available if the debtor is still in default after the time limit. It is after this moment that a creditor may apply, *mutatis mutandis*, the provisions regarding the execution of pledge rights. Thus, the creditor can sell property at auction or on his own, and receive payment out of the proceeds from the sale of the thing retained prior to other personal creditors of the debtor (i.e., lienor), or obtain ownership of the thing.[499]

B. Extinction on Other Grounds

365. A lien may be extinguished on other grounds. A lien is extinguished if the lienor provides the lienee with a commensurate security for the debt.[500] Besides, the provisions of Articles 897–899 pertaining to the grounds triggering the extinction of a pledge apply *mutatis mutandis* to lien.[501] Briefly speaking, a lien is extinguished once the subject-matter of it is destroyed save a substitute to which the rule

493. Taiwan Civil Code, Arts. 933, 888(2).
494. Taiwan Civil Code, Arts. 933, 889.
495. Taiwan Civil Code, Arts. 933, 890(2).
496. Taiwan Civil Code, Arts. 933, 892(1).
497. Taiwan Civil Code, Art. 932.
498. Taiwan Civil Code, Art. 936(1).
499. Taiwan Civil Code, Art. 936(2).
500. Taiwan Civil Code, Art. 937(1).
501. Taiwan Civil Code, Art. 937(2).

of real subrogation applies.[502] Second, since the lienee is required to keep physically possessing the thing in question, a lien shall be extinguished once it is returned to the lienor despite the debt still being outstanding; any reservation intended to preserve the efficacy of the lien is invalid.[503] However, the law makes an exception to this consequence if the lienee loses his possession unintentionally: the law gives the lienee two years to recover the thing, otherwise the lien fails.[504]

§3. Non-possessory Security Rights

366. We have seen in the foregoing sections two kinds of "possessory" security rights over movable property prescribed in the TCC. Attention must also be paid to the "non-possessory" security rights provided for in the "Chattels Security Transactions Act,"[505] a statute specially designed for creating *non-possessory* security rights over *movable and tangible* property. One of the following three legal techniques can be used to create it: (1) charge; (2) reservation of ownership clauses; and (3) trust receipt. These are collectively called "chattels security transactions,"[506] to which now we turn.

I. Creation

A. *The Mortgage over Chattels*

367. The mortgage over chattels[507] is defined as a security right granted by the mortgagor (i.e., the debtor) to the mortgagee (i.e., the creditor), but neither possession nor ownership of those chattels is required to be transferred to the latter, instead a registration of mortgage is required.[508] Metaphorically speaking, it is similar to

502. Taiwan Civil Code, Arts. 937(2), 899(1).
503. Taiwan Civil Code, Arts. 937(2), 897.
504. Taiwan Civil Code, Arts. 937(2), 898.
505. The official translation of the title of the act released by Taiwan's Ministry of Justice is "Personal Property Secured Transactions Act" (*see* http://law.moj.gov.tw). However, this is misleading, for the act applies only to movable and "tangible" property (i.e., chattels) while the term "personal property" encompasses intangible property as well (i.e., intellectual property, debt, etc.). Therefore, the term "chattel(s)" is instead adopted in this work, and the name of the act is likewise modified as follows: Chattels Security Transactions Act.
506. Chattels Security Transactions Act, Art. 2.
507. Chattels Security Transactions Act, Art. 15. A charge can also be imposed upon land; however, the term used in this case is not charge, but *diya* (*see* Taiwan Civil Code Art. 860) (as stated above, *diya* is equivalent to civil-law hypothec).
508. The official translation of the Act uses the term "mortgage of personal property" (please *see* http ://law.moj.gov.tw). But this is hardly correct. Technically speaking, the term "mortgage," according to English law, requires the ownership of a thing be transferred to the mortgagee (i.e., creditor), but the Act does not require it; the creditor only obtains a security right without any ownership title being vested in him. Furthermore, the term "personal property" is, for the same reason stated in the previous footnote, not an accurate term of art to be used in this context either. However, the work still adopts the term "mortgage."

pledge in that ownership of the thing still remains with the debtor (i.e., the mortgagor) but differs in that the debtor is allowed to continue to physically possess the thing. Therefore, the creditor (i.e., the mortgagee) does not physically possess the thing in question. Chattels are, however, not normally earmarked. Disputes thus may arise with regard to the existence of a security right between the parties. The law deals with this problem by requiring the real agreement (i.e., the granting of a security right) concluded by the parties be made in writing, otherwise the granting of the security right itself is invalid.[509] This obviously enhances evidential certainty regarding the charge granted. However, one more question still needs resolving: the effect against third parties. A mortgage, being a security right having proprietary effect, should hold good against every potential third party in the market. However, if this is strictly adhered to, the security of commerce would be seriously damaged, for a third party would be bound by the charge without any knowledge of it. The security of commerce must be promoted, and the idea is embedded in Article 5(1) of the CSTA: a mortgage, unless registered, cannot defeat a bona fide purchaser. In other words, if a charge is registered, it holds good against the whole world. The resulting effect is that the law, based on registration, *deems* everyone in the market to be a *mala fide* purchaser. To conclude, the mortgage over chattels is valid if it is made in writing, but needs registering in order to have a universally binding effect.

B. Reservation of Ownership Clauses

368. Sellers of chattels/goods are entitled, by means of reservation of ownership clauses, to postpone the passing of ownership until payment of the agreed price or a stipulated condition has been satisfied.[510] Since retaining ownership functions as a means to guarantee the debt payable, the clause is tantamount to according a security right to sellers. This results in buyers being compelled to perform their obligation(s). However, sellers under this clause do not physically possess the thing in question, and buyers do not procure the ownership to the goods transacted, but only the possession thereof. This means there is a split between a security right and possession of the subject-matter thereof, as with the case of the charge mentioned above. Therefore, the clause again must be made in writing for it to be valid, and it should be registered in order to enjoy priority over bona fide third parties.[511]

509. Chattels Security Transactions Act, Art. 5(1).

510. Chattels Security Transactions Act, Art. 26. The official translation of the Act uses the term "conditional sale" (please *see* http://law.moj.gov.tw). Unfortunately, the official translation is again controversial. Conditional sales can involve various types of conditions. The focus thus should be put on the aspect of retention of ownership, rather than that of condition, for only the former correctly shows us what the characteristic feature of this security right is.

511. Chattels Security Transactions Act, Art. 5(1).

C. Trust Receipt

369. Trust receipt, the third type of non-possessory security right, involves the following four stages:[512] (1) a person borrows money from another; (2) the borrower purchases goods/chattels with the money borrowed; (3) both parties agree that ownership to the goods purchased vests in the lender as the subject-matter of the security; and (4) the lender simultaneously creates a trust[513] allowing the borrower to hold the "possession (i.e., trust property)" of the goods[514] purchased for the benefit of the lender. As this mechanism shows, the borrower only acquires a possessory title rather than an ownership throughout, which is sufficient to induce him or her to perform his or her obligation; the lender, by having an ownership right in respect of the goods, acquires a security right. Here, we see possession is again *detached* from ownership. The need for evidence to prove this security relationship emerges. Therefore, the agreement must be made in writing for it to be valid, and it should be registered in order for creditors to be ranked ahead of bona fide third parties in the market.[515] The writing executed in this case is what we call a "trust receipt."

II. Grantors' Duties and Execution by Grantees

370. In the following, the term "grantor" denotes a debtor (i.e., a chargor, buyer, or borrower) who grants one of the aforementioned non-possessory security rights, and the term "grantee" refers to the creditor (i.e., the chargee, seller, or lender) procuring it.

A. Grantors' Duties

371. All three non-possessory security regimes share one common feature: the grantor maintains possession of the chattel offered as the subject-matter of security, and a security right is impressed on the chattel in his hand. Thus, it is not surprising to find that the law stipulates that the grantor owes a duty of care when holding and using it.[516] Furthermore, the grantor of a charge is prohibited from relocating, selling, pledging, or transferring the thing possessed.[517] The buyer, under a retention of ownership clause, is not allowed to pledge or dispose of the thing in his possession.[518] A borrower with a trust receipt is likewise debarred from relocating the thing without the lender's (i.e., the settlor's) consent, and from pledging or charging the thing in question.[519]

512. Chattels Security Transactions Act, Art. 32.
513. That is, the creditor becomes a settlor.
514. That is, the debtor becomes a trustee.
515. Chattels Security Transactions Act, Art. 5(1).
516. Chattels Security Transactions Act, Art. 12.
517. Chattels Security Transactions Act, Art. 17.
518. Chattels Security Transactions Act, Art. 28(1)(iii).
519. Chattels Security Transactions Act, Art. 34(1)(ii)(iii).

B. Execution by Grantees

372. If the grantor in any of the non-possessory security relationships defaults on full or part of payment of the debt, the grantee is entitled to repossess the thing in question.[520] However, the grantee is obliged to give notice to the grantor three days prior to the repossession of the chattel.[521] After taking possession of the property, the grantee can sell it or apply for a court auction in order to satisfy his unpaid debt. However, either the sale or the auction must be executed within thirty days of the repossession. Moreover, a period of not less than five days of public notice is required, and, finally, the grantor should be notified ten days prior to the sale or the auction.[522] The proceeds from the sale or the auction are used to satisfy the debt owed to the grantee, and any excess must be returned to the grantor.[523]

520. Chattels Security Transactions Act, Arts. 17(1), 28(1)(i), 34(1)(i).
521. Chattels Security Transactions Act, Arts. 18(1), 30, 37.
522. Chattels Security Transactions Act, Arts. 19(1), 30, 37.
523. Chattels Security Transactions Act, Arts. 20, 30, 37.

Selected Bibliography

Barry, Norman. "Property Rights in Common and Civil Law." In *The Elgar Companion to the Economics of Property Rights*, edited by Enrico Colombatto. Northampton: Edward Elgar Publishing, 2004, 177–196.

Chang, Yun-chien & Henry E. Smith. "An Economic Analysis of Civil Versus Common Law Property." *Notre Dame Law Review* 88(1) (2012): 1–55.

Chang, Yun-chien & Henry E. Smith. "The *Numerus Clausus* Principle, Property Customs, and the Emergence of New Property Forms." *Iowa Law Review* 100 (2015): 2275–2308.

Chang, Yun-chien & Lee Anne Fennell. "Partition and Revelation." *University of Chicago Law Review* 81 (2014): 27–51.

Chang, Yun-chien & Lee Anne Fennell. "Appendices to Partition and Revelation." *University of Chicago Law Review* 81, Dialogue 1 (2014): 1–13.

Chang, Yun-chien, et al. "Anchoring Effect in Real Litigations." Working Paper (2014).

Chang, Yun-chien. "An Economic and Comparative Analysis of Specificatio (the Accession Doctrine)." *European Journal of Law and Economics* 39 (2015): 225–243.

Chang, Yun-chien. "An Economic Analysis of Good-Faith Purchase of Chattels." Working Paper (2017).

Chang, Yun-chien. "An Empirical Study of Legal Servitude of Passage Cases in Taiwan." *Taiwan Law Review* 216 (2013): 211–227.

Chang, Yun-chien. "Condominium Law in Taiwan: Doctrinal Overview under the Lens of Information-Cost Theory." *Asia Pacific Law Review* 23 (2) (2015): 89–120.

Chang, Yun-chien. "Eminent Domain Law in Taiwan: New Law, Old Practice?." In *Eminent Domain: A Comparative Perspective*, edited by Iljoong Kim, Hojun Lee & Ilya Somin. (2017) : 93–117.

Chang, Yun-chien. "Empire Building and Fiscal Illusion? An Empirical Study of Government Official Behaviors in Takings." *Journal of Empirical Legal Studies* 6 (3) (2009): 541–584.

Chang, Yun-chien. "First Possession." *Taiwan Law Review* 251 (2016): 226–233.

Chang, Yun-chien. "Hybrid Rule: Hidden Entitlement Protection Rule in Access to Landlocked Land Doctrine." *Tulane Law Review* 91: 217–257 (2016).

Chang, Yun-chien. "Optional Law in Property: Theoretical Critiques and a New View of the Cathedral." *NYU Journal of Law and Liberty* 9 (2015): 459–512.

Selected Bibliography

Chang, Yun-chien. "Acquisitive Prescription of Chattels." *Taiwan Law Review* 255 (2016): 133–140.

Chang, Yun-chien. *Private Property and Takings Compensation: Theoretical Framework and Empirical Analysis*. Northampton: Edward Elgar Publishing, 2013.

Chang, Yun-chien. "Property Law with Chinese Characteristics: An Economic and Comparative Analysis." *Brigham-Kanner Property Rights Conference Journal* 1 (2012): 345–372.

Chang, Yun-chien. "Self-Assessment of Takings Compensation: An Empirical Study." *Journal of Law, Economics, and Organization* 28 (2012): 265–285.

Chang, Yun-chien. "Structure and Style of Property Law: The Case of Mortgage and Chattel Mortgage." *Taiwan Law Review* 241 (2015): 77–87.

Chang, Yun-chien. "Tenancy in 'Anticommons'?: A Theoretical and Empirical Analysis of Co-Ownership." *Journal of Legal Analysis* 4 (2012): 515–553.

Chang, Yun-chien. "The Economy of Concept and Possession." In *Law and Economics of Possession*, edited by Yun-chien Chang. Cambridge: Cambridge University Press, 2015, 103–127.

Chang, Yun-chien. "The Evolution of Property Law in Taiwan: An Unconventional Interest Group Story." In *Private Law in China and Taiwan: Economic and Legal Analyses*, edited by Yun-chien Chang, Wei Shen & Wen Yeu Wang. Cambridge: Cambridge University Press, 2016: 212–244.

Chang, Yun-chien. "The Problematic Concept of Possession in the DCFR: Lessons from *Law and Economics of Possession*." *European Property Law Journal* 5 (1) (2016): 4–25.

Chang, Yun-chien. "To Tear Down or Not to Tear Down? An Empirical Study of Building Encroachment Cases in Taiwan." In *Empirical Legal Analysis: Assessing the Performance of Legal Institutions*, edited by Yun-chien Chang. New York: Routledge, 2014, 144–158.

Chang, Yun-chien. "Venerable or Outdated? A Radical Proposal to Reform Acquisitive Prescription Law in Taiwan." *Academia Sinica Law Journal* 18 (2016): 195–266.

Ellickson, Robert C. "The Costs of Complex Land Titles: Two Examples from China." *Brigham-Kanner Property Rights Conference Journal* 1 (2011): 281–302.

Ellickson, Robert C. *The Household: Informal Order Around the Hearth*. Princeton: Princeton University Press, 2008.

Gray, Kevin & Susan Francis Gray. *Elements of Land Law*. 5th edn. Oxford: Oxford University Press, 2009.

Hinteregger, Monika. "The Protection of Property Rights." In *Cases, Materials and Text on Property Law*, edited by Sjef Van Erp & Bram Akkermans. Oxford: Hart Publishing, 2012, 97–210.

Honoré, Tony. "On Fitting Trusts into Civil Law Jurisdiction." In Oxford Legal Studies Research Paper 27 (2008). SSRN: http://ssrn.com/abstract=1270179.

Hsieh, Tsay-chuan. *Civil Code Property II*. Taipei: New Sharing Publishing, 2010.

Hsieh, Tsay-chuan. "The Amendment of the Book of Things in the Taiwan Civil Code." *Taiwan Law Review* 100 (2007): 17–33.

Huang, Chengyi & David Law. "Proportionality Review of Administrative Action in Japan, Korea, Taiwan, and China." In *Research Handbook in Comparative Law and Regulation*, edited by Francesca Bignami & David Zaring. Northampton: Edward Elgar Publishing, 2016: 305–334.

Huang, Philip C. *Code, Custom, and Legal Practice in China: The Qing and the Republic Compared*. Stanford: Stanford University Press, 2001.

Koo, Hui-Wen. "Property Rights, Land Prices, and Investment: A Study of the Taiwanese Land Registration System." *Journal of Institutional and Theoretical Economics* 167 (2011): 515–531.

Lawson, F.H. *A Common Lawyer Looks at the Civil Law*. Ann Arbor: Michigan Law School, 1955.

McFarlane, Ben. *The Structure of Property Law*. Oxford: Hart Publishing, 2008.

Merrill, Thomas W. "Accession and Original Ownership." *Journal of Legal Analysis* 1 (2009): 459–510.

Merrill, Thomas W. & Henry E. Smith. "The Property/Contract Interface." *Columbia Law Review* 101 (2001): 773–852.

Miceli, Thomas J., C.F. Sirmans & Geoffrey K. Turnbull. "The Property-Contract Boundary: An Economic Analysis of Leases." *American Law and Economics Review* 3 (2001): 165–185.

Schurmann, H.F. "Traditional Property Concepts in China." *Journal of Asian Studies* 15 (1956): 507–516.

Swadling, William. "Property: General Principles." In *English Private Law*, edited by Andrew Burrow. 2nd edn. Oxford: Oxford University Press, 2008, 219–401.

Tan Sook Yee, Tang Hang Wu & Kelvin F.K. Low. *Tan Sook Yee's Principles of Singapore Land Law*. 3rd edn. Singapore: LexisNexis, 2009.

Wang, Tay-Sheng, Hua-Yuan Hsueh & Wen-Jie Huang. *Traces of Taiwan Law History*. Taipei: Wu-Nan Cultural Enterprise, 2006.

Wang, Tay-Sheng. "The Legal Development of Taiwan in the 20th Century: Toward a Liberal and Democratic Country." *Pacific Rim and Policy* 11 (2002): 531–559.

Wang, Tay-Sheng. "Translation, Codification and Transplantation of Foreign Laws in Taiwan." *Washington International Law Journal* 25 (2) (2016): 307–329.

Wang, Wen-Yeu, Chieh-Cheng Wang & Jer-Sheng Shieh. "Trust Law in Taiwan: History, Current Features and Future Prospects." In *Trust Law in Asian Civil Law Jurisdictions: A Comparative Analysis*, edited by Lusina Ho & Rebecca Lee. Oxford: Oxford University Press, 2013, 63–79.

Wu, Kuang-ming. *New Civil Code Property*. Taipei: San Min Publishing, 2009.

WU, Ying-Chieh. "East Asian Trusts at the Crossroads." *National Taiwan University Law Review* 10 (1) (2015): 79–124.

WU, Ying-Chieh. "Trust Law in South Korea: Developments and Challenges." In *Trust Law in Asian Civil Law Jurisdictions: A Comparative Analysis*, edited by Lusina Ho & Rebecca Lee. Oxford: Oxford University Press, 2013, 46–62.

Zhang, Taisu. "Property Rights in Land, Agricultural Capitalism, and the Relative Decline of Pre-Industrial China." *San Diego International Law Journal* 13 (2011): 129–200.

Selected Bibliography

Table of Cases and Statutes

Statutes

Dongchan Danbao Jiaoyi Fa [Chattels Security Transactions Act].
Gong Yu Da Sha Guan Li Tiao Li [Condominium Administration Act].
Guotu Jihua Fa [The Act for National Land Use Planning].
Guoyou Caichan Fa [The Act for State-owned Assets].
Haishang Fa [The Maritime Law].
Min Fa [Taiwan Civil Code].
Tu Di Fa [Land Act].
Tu Di Zheng Shou Tiao Li [Land Expropriation Act].
Wenhua Zichan Baohu Fa [Cultural Heritage Preservation Act].
Xintuo Fa [Trust Act].
Yuanzhumin Jiben Fa [Regulations of Aboriginal Clan Reservation Development and Management].
Zhongyang Fagui Biaozhun Fa [Standard Act for Law and Rules].

Enforcement Rules

Gong Yu Da Sha Guan Li Tiao Li Shi Xing Xi Ze [Enforcement Rules for the Condominium Administration Act].
Tu Di Zheng Shou Bu Chang Shi Jia Cha Gu Ban Fa [Regulations on Appraising Current Market Value for Takings Compensation].
Tu Di Zheng Shou Tiao Li Shi Xing Xi Ze [Enforcement Rules for the Land Expropriation Act].

Supreme Court

Zui Gao Fa Yuan [Supreme Court] 6th Civil Resolution Meeting of Year 1974.
Zui Gao Fa Yuan [Supreme Court] 2nd Civil Resolution Meeting of Year 1978.
Zui Gao Fa Yuan 41 Nian Tai Shang Zi Di 1039 Hao Pan Li [Supreme Court 1952 No. 1039 Precedent].
Zui Gao Fa Yuan 48 Nian Tai Shang Zi Di 1812 Hao Pan Li [Supreme Court 1959 No. 1812 Precedent].
Zui Gao Fa Yuan 50 Nian Tai Shang Zi Di 1236 Hao Pan Li [Supreme Court 1961 No. 1236 Precedent].
Zui Gao Fa Yuan 52 Nian Tai Shang Zi Di 681 Hao Pan Li [Supreme Court 1963 No. 681 Precedent].

Zui Gao Fa Yuan 69 Nian Tai Shang Zi Di 3726 Hao Pan Li [Supreme Court 1980 No. 3726 Precedent].
Zui Gao Fa Yuan 80 Nian Tai Shang Zi Di 804 Hao Pan Jue [Supreme Court 1991 No. 804 Decision].

High Court

Tai Wan Gao Deng Fa Yuan Tai Zhong Fen Yuan 96 Nian Du Zhong Zai Geng (1) Zi Di 1 Hao Min Shi Pan Jue [High Court 2007 No. 1 Decision].
Tai Wan Gao Deng Fa Yuan Tai Nan Fen Yuan 100 Nian Du Shang Zi Di 250 Hao Min Shi Pan Jue [High Court 2011 No. 250 Decision].
Tai Wan Gao Deng Fa Yuan Tai Nan Fen Yuan 102 Nian Du Shang Yi Zi Di 21 Hao Min Shi Pan Jue [High Court 2013 No. 21 Decision].

District Court

Tai Wan Tai Nan Di Fang Fa Yuan 91 Nian Du Su Zi Di 1944 Hao Min Shi Pan Jue [District Court 2002 No. 1994 Decision].
Tai Wan Tai Bei Di Fang Fa Yuan 95 Nian Du Bei Jian Zi Di 57353 Hao Min Shi Jian Yi Pan Jue [District Court 2006 No. 57353 Decision].
Tai Wan Tai Bei Di Fang Fa Yuan 96 Nian Du Jian Shang Zi Di 111 Hao Min Shi Pan Jue [District Court 2007 No. 111 Decision].
Tai Wan Tai Nan Di Fang Fa Yuan 99 Nian Du Su Zi Di 1672 Hao Min Shi Pan Jue [District Court 2010 No. 1672 Decision].
Tai Wan Gao Xiong Di Fang Fa Yuan 99 Nian Du Xiong Jian Zi Di 2056 Hao Min Shi Pan Jue [District Court 2010 No. 2056 Decision].
Tai Wan Tai Bei Di Fang Fa Yuan 100 Nian Du Su Zi Di 3156 Hao Min Shi Pan Jue [District Court 2011 Appeal No. 3156 Decision].
Tai Wan Gao Xiong Di Fang Fa Yuan 100 Nian Du Feng Jian Zi Di 721 Hao Min Shi Pan Jue [District Court 2011 No. 721 Decision].
Tai Wan Gao Xiong Di Fang Fa Yuan 101 Nian Du Jian Shang Zi Di 281 Hao Min Shi Pan Jue [District Court 2012 No.281 Decision].
Tai Wan Shi Lin Di Fang Fa Yuan 101 Nian Du Su Zi Di 111 Hao Min Shi Pan Jue [District Court 2012 Appeal No. 111 Decision].
Tai Wan Xin Bei Di Fang Fa Yuan 102 Nian Du Su Zi Di 1416 Hao Min Shi Pan Jue [District Court 2013 Appeal No. 1416 Decision].
Tai Wan Gao Xiong Di Fang Fa Yuan 102 Nian Du Su Zi Di 1891 Hao Min Shi Pan Jue [District Court 2013 Appeal No. 1891 Decision].

Shih Tzu [Interpretation of Council of Grand Justices]

No. 93.
No. 107
No. 110
No. 139
No. 154
No. 215
No. 236
No. 291
No. 336

No. 349
No. 350
No. 400
No. 408
No. 409
No. 425
No. 440
No. 451
No. 508
No. 513
No. 516
No. 534
No. 579
No. 652

Index

[We list terms in both English and Chinese here and order them alphabetically. Please kindly note that in this index we translate Chinese legal terms into English rather than translating legal terms in English into Chinese.]
The numbers here refer to paragraph numbers.

Index

www.ingramcontent.com/pod-product-compliance
Ingram Content Group UK Ltd.
Pitfield, Milton Keynes, MK11 3LW, UK
UKHW020145290926
15471UKWH00004B/707

9 789403 548401